# FEELING
## God's Presence Today

*Begin each day with a sensory experience
from God to you*

© 2010 Laine Lawson Craft

Published by WHOA Ministries

Edited by Amy Braud-Wallace

ISBN 978-0-615-38179-4

www.whoaministries.com
www.lainelawsoncraft.net
www.lainecraftbooks.com

Cover and interior design, Amy Braud-Wallace

Printed in China by RR Donnelley

Many have asked me, "How did you find God on such an intimate level?' The best answer I can give is that I had a sensual experience with God. I felt his touch literally one desperate night of despair that embraced my broken heart, I heard his voice that tiny quiet voice deep within my soul that told me knowledge that could not come from me, I saw his glory in miraculous results in my personal life, I tasted victory when God exalted me into ministry, and became a sweet fragrance to him as I surrendered my entire life to him.

My motivation to this 365 day daily devotional book was to help you find God on a sensory level too. My passion is to show all that God is readily available, real, and longing to touch us an intimate way. Through these scriptures that touch on the five senses I tried to give application to help you feel a sensual feeling from God so that you too will have a deeper more meaningful relationship with God.

*"New Mercies Everyday"*
*Photography by Laine Lawson Craft*

Begin each day with a "sensory experience" from God to you! Drawn from the actual word of God each of these 365 devotions includes a Scripture verse, inspirational reading, and prayer starter. Discover how you can feel the presence of God knowing that He can reach you through all five senses. This can transform the way you approach your life!

My sincere thanks to many who have played a major part of my life that brings God all the glory.

My husband, Steve, who has given me grace, mercy, and love that emulates God's example.

My children, Steven, Lawson, and Kaylee who lovingly support me when they know God has called me to do his work and who always make me feel loved even when God calls me away.

My parents, Earl and Shirlee Lawson, my ninety-five year old grandparents, Jerry and A.G. Tye, and my four siblings, Vickie, Ronda, Aleesa, and Al, and the many nieces, nephews, great-nieces, in-laws, and to my many dear friends - you know who you are.

Thank you to my new found friend and editor, Amy Braud-Wallace who had faith in me.

To God be all the GLORY for rescuing me and making me whole and righteous through the blood of his son, Jesus, who offers us all an intimate relationship right where we are and just the way God made us!

Genesis 3:8

*And they heard the sound of the Lord God walking in the garden in the cool of the day, and Adam and his wife hid themselves from the presence of the Lord God among the trees of the garden.*

How amazing would it be to actually hear God walk beside us? Adam and Eve heard God coming. When we talk with God, are we allowing ourselves to be completely open, deep in our hearts and minds, to hear God approaching us?

Today we must challenge ourselves to expand our definitions on what God can do today. Let's listen for God coming closer to us.

Dear God, Please give me new ears to hear you in an entirely different way than I have in the past. Please today, let me hear you in a way that I know it is you. Whether it be a whisper or a loud clap, I believe I will hear you today as never before. Thank you I love you.

*Day 2*

<u>Genesis 21:17</u>
*And God heard the voice of the youth,*

Sometimes I think we all wonder and ponder if God really hears us? Does God hear our cries? Does He hear our despair? Particularly, I wonder does He hear my children's cries and needs that they pray to him.

In this verse we see that God definitely hears the cry of the youth. God throughout scripture made it clear that children are his heart. God even challenges us that we must become like a child to enter his Kingdom.

Today, if you have children, tell them confidently that God hears every word they bring to him. Encourage them to ask God for whatever they may need. For you, become more childlike when you come before God.

Dear God, Let my children know you hear them. Answer their prayers Lord. Help me too, Lord, to become more childlike in your presence. Thanks, Lord. I love you.

Genesis 30:6

*And Rachel said, God has judged and vindicated me, and has heard my plea and has given me a son;*

Many of us have gone to God with a specific plea. Maybe today you have something that you must have answered to carry on. As Rachel experienced, God heard her and gave her what she needed.

Many of us have not because we ask not. Today, ask God for the one thing you must get and believe with all your heart it will be answered.

Dear God, I have many needs but specifically today, I need an answer to this _____. Lord, I believe that you will answer me and I will know that today you are with me by the answers you give to me. I love you and Thank you in advance for this _____. I love you. Amen.

*Day 4*

<u>Exodus 2:24</u>
*And God heard their sighing and groaning
and [earnestly] remembered His covenant
with Abraham, with Isaac, and with Jacob.*

God is a God that will never lie or go back
on his promises to his children. Sometimes
when we cry out to the Lord He is moved
to remind himself to past promises. God
will always back up his promises to us.

Today, make a list of promises you need
fulfilled from God. Then, go to God and
one by one read them and apply them to
your personal needs and desires. God loves
to be reminded of his promises because
that shows our steadfast trust in his word!

Dear God, you are a God of Trust and
Covenants to your children. Please, Lord,
I remind you of the promises you made
and how my life needs you to fulfill them
today. I know you are a God that does not
lie. Please help me to have assurance you
hear my groans and meet my needs. Thank
you Lord, I love you.

Deuteronomy 4:10

*Especially how on the day that you stood*
*before the Lord your God in Horeb,*
*the Lord said to me, Gather the people*
*together to Me and I will make them hear*
*My words, that they may learn [reverently]*
*to fear Me all the days they live upon*
*the earth and that they may teach their*
*children.*

What words are we teaching our children
today? Do they hear us proclaim who God
is? Do they see us praying to God?

We must teach our children who God is
and to reverently fear him. To fear God is
to know him and to learn from him. What
are we saying in front of our children that
demonstrates to them how to hear God's
words?

Dear God, help me to show my children
who you are by the words I speak. Lord,
I know you hear my words. Lord, let me
help my children hear your words and to
reverently fear you so that they too can
learn from you. Love you. Amen

*Day 6*

<u>Deuteronomy 5:24</u>
*And you said, Behold, the Lord our God has shown us His glory and His greatness, and we have heard His voice out of the midst of the fire; we have this day seen that God speaks with man and man still lives.*

Many read this and say, "Can God really speak to me?" YES! The Lord speaks all the time, but are you hearing him? It is a glorious thing to know that God has spoken to you.

Many ask me, "How do you hear God?" The best way to explain is when something is pressed on you, a thought, a person, or even idea, and it will not go away. Many times this is the Lord speaking to you. The next time you have something that will not let go of you, do it. You will see the Lord.

Dear God, let me have ears to hear you speak. Nudge me today to do something, so I can see that you do speak to me. Thank you. I love you.

Deuteronomy 5:24

*And you said, Behold, the Lord our God has shown us His glory and His greatness, and we have heard His voice out of the midst of the fire; we have this day seen that God speaks with man and man still lives.*

The next time you are in a heated moment like an argument, stop, and listen. Many times God will show up in places where you would least expect him. But, you must stop and then, listen.

Next time you are in a heated and fiery situation, stop. Then, just listen to that ever so small voice deep within you. God will speak, and you will hear it. Don't let the fire keep you from being cool, calm, and collected, ready to hear from God.

Dear God, please help me today in the heat of life's struggles just to stop. Lord, help me to listen at the unlikeliest times of my days. Don't let the fire of life's trials keep me from being a cool spirit of God. I love you. Amen.

*Day 8*

<u>Deuteronomy 5:27</u>
*Go near [Moses] and hear all that the Lord our God will say. And speak to us all that the Lord our God will speak to you; and we will hear and do it.*

How many of us go to church, Bible Study, or small group to hear God's word, and leave unchanged? How many of us actually hear the word and allow it to move us? Do we hear the word and obey it?

Faith is hearing, obeying, and acting on God's word. Today, read some scripture and ask God to move you and change you so that you will act on what it is God is telling you to do. Let the words and scriptures speak to us and motivate us to act on what we hear from God.

Dear God, let me hear you in a different way today. Let me hear your words and it change me in such a way others see you. Let my actions be a direct result of hearing you speak to me today. I love you. Amen

Deuteronomy 6:4
*Hear, O Israel: the Lord our God is one Lord [the only Lord].*

Many today tell us there is more than one God or more than one Lord. ABSOLUTELY NOT! There is only one Lord and one God. Do not get swallowed up in the world's opinion of other gods.

God is the only God. Don't be fooled. The enemy wants us to accept Allah, Buddha, and many more other gods. DO NOT be influenced by these false prophets.

God is the only Lord -the Master and the Creator of all. He truly is the beginning and the end, the Alpha and the Omega. Do not be misled or misinformed. Our God is one Lord.

Dear God keep my ears tuned in only to you today. Let me have the confidence that you are the only one true God and that there is no other God. Don't let me deny this truth with the deception of acceptance of other's gods. I love you. Amen.

*Day 10*

<u>Deuteronomy 26:7</u>
*And when we cried to the Lord, the God of our fathers, the Lord heard our voice and looked on our affliction and our labor and our [cruel] oppression;*

Some of you are under oppression today. The enemy has so much going on in your life, you feel as though you are drowning. Some of you are afflicted with physical ailments and emotional trials. CRY OUT to the Lord!

Confidently cry out right now and say Lord, you must show up today and hear my cry. The Lord will answer. He will hear your voice and break you free from oppression and afflictions. Believe it and cry out.

Dear God, hear my voice and my desperate cry for help today. Break the chains of oppression and the burden of afflictions and emotional stress. Lord, let me see you today as you answer my cries. I love you. Amen

Deuteronomy 31:13
*And that their children, who have not
known it, may hear and learn [reverently]
to fear the Lord your God as long as you
live in the land which you go over the
Jordan to possess.*

What is it that you are trying to achieve?
Jordan seemed almost impossible to cross.
They never dreamed they could possess the
land across from the Jordan. What is your
Jordan today, a troubled child or a failing
marriage?

Let your children know your fears and hear
your prayers to the Lord. Let them see the
power of God who hears and answers us.
Give God your Jordan today and share this
with your kids. Allow them the honor of
seeing God work in supernatural ways in
your life.

Dear God I give to my Jordan today. Lord
I know you hear my cries and know my
needs. I know that you will help me to
cross the Jordan, and my children will
know and learn from it. I love you. Amen.

*Day 12*

<u>1 Samuel 9:27</u>
*And as they were going down to the outskirts of the city, Samuel said to Saul, Bid the servant pass on before us - and he passed on - but you stand still, first, that I may cause you to hear the word of God.*

Many of us are seldom still. This world we live in today moves at such a pace many feel as if they are in a race every moment. TOO FAST, too furious, are the terms we live by today.

We must slow down and stand still. That is the only way we will hear God above all of the chaos the world gives us everyday. We must hear God's word so that we may live in the ways He has planned for us.

Dear God please help me to slow down, not just for today but for a lifetime. Lord, help me change my pace to a new lifestyle where I stand still so that I can hear you speak. Thank you Lord, I love you. Amen.

<u>2 Samuel 7:22</u>
*Therefore You are great, O Lord God;*
*for none is like You, nor is there any God*
*besides You, according to all [You have*
*made] our ears to hear.*

God, help us today to acknowledge that
there is none like you. There is no other
God but you! You have made us your
creation to hear your voice. Lord, help us
to hear you as you would have us to do.

Lord, help me to remove anything in my
life that keeps me from hearing you. Lord,
help me to know when you are speaking to
me. We all need to make sure that we stand
still again today so that we are able to hear.
Thank you who created us with the ability
to hear because it would be impossible to
make it with out hearing you speak.

Lord, let me open my ears to hear you
in a unique way. Lord, there is none like
you. You created us so that we could hear
you. Thank you for our ears. I love you.
Amen.

*Day 14*

<u>1 Samuel 12:14</u>

*If you will revere and fear the Lord and serve Him and hearken to His voice and not rebel against His commandment, and if both you and your king will follow the Lord your God, it will be good!*

All of us are guilty of rebelling against God. Why has God made us so stubborn? Not one person I have ever met has enjoyed being told what to do. Most of us do the opposite of what we are told to do.

It's clear that rebellion does not work with God. Life is much easier if we just hear God's commandments and obey. We must serve him and do as He instructs so that we will have a good life. Today, we must let go of any rebellious spirit holding us back from obeying God's word.

Father, please forgive my rebellious spirit. Deliver me in the name and blood of Jesus to hear your commandments and obey you so I can have a good life. I love you. Amen

2 Samuel 22:7

*In my distress I called upon the Lord; I cried to my God, and He heard my voice from His temple; my cry came into His ears.*

I am reminded of a stress call, like an SOS you send when you're in trouble. Or, if you hear a tornado warning siren like we do here in the South. I feel strongly that God hears the cries of distress more clearly than ever. God loves to help us!

As I read this scripture, the fact that God has ears brought a new revelation. We are made in his image, and I wondered, "Do his ears look like ours?" Does God actually have a distress call mechanism that alerts him of our cries of need and help? No matter how God hears our cries of distress, He answers all of our prayers of need.

Thank you Lord for the assurance you hear our voices and cries of distress. Thank you for making us in your image. Lord we love you, thank you for hearing us. Amen

<u>2 Chronicles 33:13</u>
*He prayed to Him, and God, entreated by him, heard his supplication and brought him again to Jerusalem to his kingdom. Then Manasseh knew that the Lord is God.*

The word "entreated" means to beg or to earnestly ask for something. God heard the earnest request. Do we come to God with earnest needs and thoughtful prayer requests? Or do we just immediately go to God for anything we want without true thought?

Supplication is humbling. Do we humbly go before God with our needs? Today let's all go to God with an earnest prayer request with a humble heart and watch God work on our behalf.

Lord, forgive me for just throwing prayers up without any real thought. Lord, please forgive my prideful heart too. Lord, I humbly ask that you answer this request _____, and Lord, I thank you for hearing me. I love you. Amen.

<u>Job 33:15</u>
*[One may hear God's voice] in a dream, in a vision of the night, when deep sleep falls on men while slumbering upon the bed,*

When I read this verse, I immediately knew why God so often speaks to us in our sleep. When we are sleeping, that is sometimes the only time that we are completely still. Also, when He wakes us or gives us a dream, we know that something beyond our physical abilities is occurring.

I ask God to visit me in dreams and to awaken me and speak so I can hear him clearly. Today, why don't you do the same? Ask God to give you dreams and awaken you to hear just his voice.

Dear God, please come to me in my sleep. While I rest, you come, wake me up, and speak to me. Or, give me a dream that I can better understand who you are. I love you. Amen

<u>Job 33:19</u>
*[God's voice may be heard by man when]*
*he is chastened with pain upon his bed and*
*with continual strife in his bones or while*
*all his bones are firmly set,*

This makes me sad for those who don't
know the Lord until their health is failing.
I feel grateful that I hear God's voice
without being in pain and bedridden.

Don't wait until you have to hear from
God. Go to him today and ask him to give
you health and to give you ears so that can
clearly hear him. You don't want to have to
be stricken with pain in order to line your
life up enough with God's plan so that you
can hear him.

Dear God, Thank you for my health today.
Thank you that I can feel you within a
grateful heart of health. Lord, let me hear
you in the good times and particularly the
bad times of life. I love you. Amen

Psalm 17:6
*I have called upon You, O God, for You will hear me; incline Your ear to me and hear my speech.*

Lord, I do call upon you today. I need to talk with you about all that is going on in my life. Lord, there are so many things I don't understand. I long to hear the words you would speak. Lord, please incline your ear to me.

What strength I find in knowing that you know who I am and that you would lean towards me to hear me better. Lord, let me speak with you in honesty of despair and hopelessness today. Please Lord, speak into my pain.

Lord, please hear my pain. Lord, answer me today in ways that I know it can only be you. Lord, thank you for loving me enough to come closer to me in my despair and pain. Remove oh Lord, this from me today, the heavy heart. I love you. Amen.

Psalm 50:7
*Hear, O My people, and I will speak; O
Israel, I will testify to you and against you:
I am God, your God.*

Be careful today because God will speak
and nothing will hold him back! God is
God, and He will have what He desires for
us. Ask yourself today, "Am I on the good
side of God or the bad side of God?"

God will stand either with you or against
you. God can not be anywhere that sin
exists. SO today, you must choose whether
God would testify against you or for you.

Dear God, please forgive me and allow me
to be within your compass of care. Lord,
please testify for me that I do love you.
Lord, please help me to be a better person
and a better example of what you are in my
life today. Forgive me today, Lord, so that
I will know you are with me. I love you.
Amen.

Psalm 62:11
*God has spoken once, twice have I heard this: that power belongs to God.*

How many of us today feel like we are in control of our lives, our children, our jobs, our families, and our money? How many of us try to control the future life that we will have? Many of us try and think that we are in control. WRONG!

God is the power. God is in complete control of our everyday lives as well as our future. Surrender today to him and give the control back to God. Tell God He is in control of every aspect of your life.

Dear God, please forgive me for trying to control all things in my life. Lord, I will listen closer to you for instructions for my life. I know today that I give you my life, my dreams, and all that I am to you. I love you. Amen

*Day 22*

<u>Psalm 66:19</u>
*But certainly God has heard me; He has given heed to the voice of my prayer.*

Heed is to give careful attention. WHOA! This humbles me to the core that God the God of all the universe pays close attention to my prayers. Many of us don't give ourselves enough worth when it comes to God.

God, the word explains, has certainly heard us. God has paid careful attention to the petitions of our needs. This is amazing. Today, just know that God really does care for you, that He hears and pays close attention to our prayers.

Dear Father, I love you and I thank you for hearing me. Lord, forgive me when I doubt. Thank you for being a God of certainty and the one upon whom I can always count. I love you, and thank you for hearing me when I pray. Amen.

<u>Psalm 77:1</u>
*I WILL cry to God with my voice, even to
God with my voice, and He will give ear
and hearken to me.*

Isn't this is a great affirmation that God
hears ours cries? I have learned to really
go before the Lord to sound out my heart's
pain. Crying out to God on a deep personal
level has brought me so much closer to
him. There are no games, no manipulations,
just tears of despair and needs.

God not only hears our cry but He hearkens
to us. Hearken means to heed, to pay close
attention to. How incredible to know God
is that close to my heart. The enemy makes
us think that the pain and heartaches are
caused by God, but it is not true. God is not
only listening to our cries, He cries with us.

Dear God, I know you hear my cries and
you heed to them. Lord I cry out today and
feel your presence as you comfort my pain.
Lord help me to come to you more often in
a broken state, so I can grow closer to you.
I love you. Amen.

Psalm 78:59
*When God heard this, He was full of [holy]
wrath; and He utterly rejected Israel,
greatly abhorring and loathing [her ways],*

This shows me God is a God with
righteous anger. He will reject those who
do not hear him and obey. He watches
patiently as we ignore him, but only for a
certain time.

God can not watch us sin and be silent
forever. There is a time when God must
show his wrath and anger to those who do
not hear him. Are you doing as God ask
us to do? Are we living a life that He can
watch and not loathe?

Today, ask God to make your life one that
He can watch and gladly speak into your
ways.

Dear God, please forgive me in all of my
sin. Lord, please forgive me if I ever bring
you into wrath or loathing me. I love you,
and today, I ask you to make my life one
that you can be a part of. Amen.

Proverbs 28:9

*He who turns away his ear from hearing the law [of God and man], even his prayer is an abomination, hateful and revolting [to God].*

My challenge to all is to turn to God and not from God. Either we are drawing closer to God in our lives, or we are pulling further from Him. Are you coming closer to God?

God says here that if we turn our ear from Him, it is revolting to Him. God will not listen. As followers of Christ, we must listen for God and then do what He has asked of us. Otherwise the worst can happen. God will turn from us, and our prayers will be an abomination to him.

Dear God today I draw closer to you. Lord I am turning toward you today. I need you. I do not want you to turn away from me or to have my prayers be an abomination to you. I love you. Amen.

<u>Isaiah 38:5</u>
*Go, and say to Hezekiah, Thus says the
Lord, the God of David your father: I have
heard your prayer, I have seen your tears;
behold, I will add to your life fifteen years.*

God can do anything! He not only hears
our prayers then answers them, He adds 15
years to our lives! God sees every tear that
falls from our cheeks. God hears every cry
to him. Then, God makes the impossible
happen.

What man can't do, like add 15 years to
our lives, God can do. God is amazing. He
hears us, sees our tears, and then does the
supernatural in answering them to show his
GLORY!

Dear God, thank you for seeing every tear
that falls from my eyes. Thank you for
hearing every prayer of need and pain.
Lord,  I ask you today to supernaturally
answer this prayer of need, _____,
so that I can tell all of your glory through
my life and answered prayers!

<u>Jeremiah 19:15</u>
*Thus says the Lord of hosts, the God of Israel: Behold, I will bring upon this city and upon all its towns all the evil that I have pronounced against it, because they have stiffened their necks, refusing to hear My words.*

God will NOT tolerate an unopened heart. Your ears feed the heart. If you do not open your ears to hear the Lord, then you will succumb to evil. If you refuse God, then He will release you to your own demise.

Don't stiffen your neck to God. When your life gets overwhelming and too much to bear, instead of running, go to him and cry out. Then wait patiently for his answer. You know God hears our cries and prayers.

God, please help me to run to you rather than to run away from you. Lord, help me not to get angry with you when life gets too hard. Lord, please don't let me stiffen my neck because I don't want to refuse your words and live in evil. I love you. Amen.

<u>Ezekiel 3:27</u>
*But when I speak with you, I will open your
mouth and you shall say to the people,
Thus says the Lord God; he who hears, let
him hear, and he who refuses to hear, let
him refuse; for they are a rebellious house.*

The Lord not only hears our prayers, but
He uses us to speak to those who need to
hear from him! God will put the words
right into our mouths if we allow him when
He needs to tell something.

Don't close your mouth or your ears to
the Lord. You do not want to live in a
rebellious house! Listen for God. Hear God
when He speaks. Then, allow God to use
your mouth to get the message out to
those whom He needs to tell something.

Dear God, use my mouth today. Allow me
to be your mouthpiece to someone today
who needs affirmation that you do indeed
hear his or her prayers. Lord let me never
live in a rebellious house, and never let my
ears to refuse to hear you speak. Lord, I
love you. Amen.

Ezekiel 10:5
*And the sound of the wings of the cherubim was heard even to the outer court, like the voice of God Almighty when He speaks.*

What amazes me is that some can actually hear God speak. God's voice is audible to some. Have you heard God speak out loud? If not, do you believe God can speak to where it can be heard?

Today we should all ask God to break down the religious spirit and wrong teachings that we aren't able to hear you today in the 21ˢᵗ century. Lord let our ears hear your speaking voice aloud if it be your will.

Dear God, please forgive me for not believing that you can speak audibly today. Please break the spirit of religion off of me in the name of Jesus and the blood of Christ and let my heart and ears be receptive to hear your voice audibly if it is your will. I love you. Amen.

<u>Zechariah 13:9</u>
*And I will bring the third part through the fire, and will refine them as silver is refined and will test them as gold is tested. They will call on My name, and I will hear and answer them. I will say, It is My people; and they will say, The Lord is my God.*

Many of us are in times of testing today. God is refining us and testing us as gold is tested. Are you calling out to him during these tests? He is the only way to turn. You can't turn to man and his devices, they will never bring what you need for eternal life.

Call out to God by name and pray, and He will answer you. He will call you his people. God will give you an answer, and you will tell others that God is your Lord because of what He has done for you.

Lord, as I am being tested please let my broken heart come before you. Lord, please forgive me for trying to run or find any other answers other than you. Lord, refine me so that I can share to others who you are - the God who answers prayers! I love you. Amen

<u>Matthew 13:17</u>
*Truly I tell you, many prophets and*
*righteous men [men who were upright and*
*in right standing with God] yearned to see*
*what you see, and did not see it, and to*
*hear what you hear, and did not hear it.*

Don't take for granted all that we have
today! God has given us so much to learn
from and to believe with all of your heart.
We have the Bible which will answer and
instruct every area of our lives.

Are you reading the word everyday? Are
you seeking God in all of your ways? Don't
miss him! Don't think for one minute you
have to be a certain way for you to see God.
Many prophets could not see what you can
see or hear!

Dear God, let me see you and hear you.
Don't let me miss you today! Now I know
that all of us are able to see and hear if we
are willing. I love you. Amen.

*Day 32*

<u>Matthew 13:43</u>
*Then will the righteous (those who are upright and in right standing with God) shine forth like the sun in the kingdom of their Father. Let him who has ears [to hear] be listening, and let him consider and perceive and understand by hearing.*

The righteous are the ones who are in right standing with God. We will shine like the sun in the Kingdom of God. Our dark world needs this desperately.

Let your ears be listening. God will show the meaning of many things to those who hear him. The only understanding of this life can come through the hearing of God's words.

Lord, let me be a sun, a ray of light that will shine your glory in this dark cold world. Lord, let me be willing to hear you and to understand all that you give to me. Lord, keep me in right standing before you. I love you. Amen

<u>Luke 11:28</u>
*But He said, Blessed (happy and to be envied) rather are those who hear the Word of God and obey and practice it!*

We don't want to be just hearers of the word. We want to be ones upon whom God can depend to do what we hear. Faith without works is dead. We want to be people who do what we hear God instruct.

Today we need to show God that He can trust us to hear him and that we will obediently do what we has told us. WHOA! Then in turn He will bless our obedience.

Dear God, please do not let me just be a hearer of the word. Lord, help me to do as you have commanded us. Lord, you can trust me to listen to your voice and act on what I hear. Lord, I want to be the hands and feet of Christ for you today. I love you. Amen.

John 5:25

*Believe Me when I assure you, most solemnly I tell you, the time is coming and is here now when the dead shall hear the voice of the Son of God and those who hear it shall live.*

Do we really want to wait until we are dead to hear God? I know He is speaking about past believers who have died, but I what I mean is "spiritually" dead? Are you waiting for something to speak to you other than God?

There is a time when the world will end. Are you ready? Do you have a personal relationship with God that allows you to hear his voice? If not, it is time to dig deeper and to hear what God is trying to tell you.

Lord, today I ask to have a deeper relation-ship with you. Lord, I ask you to draw me into your arms like never before. Lord, whisper to me and speak to me so that I know you are mine. I love you. Amen.

<u>John 8:47</u>
*Whoever is of God listens to God. [Those who belong to God hear the words of God.] This is the reason that you do not listen [to those words, to Me]: because you do not belong to God and are not of God or in harmony with Him.*

Before I knew different, I used to say all the time that I just don't hear from God. But then, I learned something new.

The next time you hear a sermon, listen to the words or voice behind what you hear. What is it that you interpreted as you heard the sermon? That is God speaking just to you! Try it next time when you listen as someone preaches or teaches and hear the words that you interpret. That will be God speaking just to you.

Thank you Lord that I hear you. Thank you that I live in harmony of all that you have created. Lord, let me never be a person who does not hear you for I know that means that we are separated. I love you. Amen.

<u>Acts 2:33</u>
*Being therefore lifted high by and to the right hand of God, and having received from the Father the promised [blessing which is the] Holy Spirit, He has made this outpouring which you yourselves both see and hear.*

The Holy Spirit is the helper that Jesus left with all believers. It is the tiny voice inside of us. The Holy Spirit gives wisdom and knowledge. The Holy Spirit enables us to see and hear God in a supernatural way.

Thank you, Lord, for the counselor and helper called the Holy Spirit. Thank you for allowing us to receive the power from it. Thank you, Lord, for the outpouring of your love when you gave us the Holy Spirit.

Dear God, thank you for our helper inside of us - the Holy Spirit. Greater is He that lives within us than he that is in the world. Thank you for the Spirit that hears and sees you. I love you. Amen.

Romans 2:13
*For it is not merely hearing the Law [read]
that makes one righteous before God, but
it is the doers of the Law who will be held
guiltless and acquitted and justified.*

Many of us would be found guilty of being
mere hearers of the word. So many think
that if you read the word that you are
fulfilling all you need to do. Many go to
church, bible study, small groups, and hear
the word. God says we must be doers of
the word.

We must put God's words into actions.
God is counting on us to show and tell the
world who He is. You can't do that without
action. You can't just read the word and
keep it to yourself!

Dear God, help me today to be bolder with
what I know I need to put into action. Let
me be a doer of your word. Lord, help
others see who you are, your glory, by the
deeds and actions of love that you have me
do for you.

Romans 11:8

*As it is written, God gave them a spirit (an attitude) of stupor, eyes that should not see and ears that should not hear, [that has continued] down to this very day.*

Don't be one of the ones who God causes not to hear him. Don't be caught up in a stupor. Stupor can mean to be stupid. Don't be stupid!

There will be those who will not hear God's voice. There will be those who do not see God in anything. This is as true today as it was in the biblical times. Don't be dismayed or persuaded to follow any of these. Know that God speaks and that you can see him in all the splendor of the earth.

Lord, please be with those who do not see or hear you. Lord, they will be in the eternal fire of Hell. Lord, keep me safe and far from those people so that I do not fall a trap of stupidity. I love you. Amen.

Philippians 4:9
*Practice what you have learned and
received and heard and seen in me, and
model your way of living on it, and the God
of peace (of untroubled, undisturbed well-
being) will be with you.*

I want to do this everyday. I want to
practice all that I know that God is! I want
all that I meet or that I see on a regular
basis, to see that I am a Christ Follower.
Let them see it not in the words I speak but
in the way I act and treat others.

Lord, let me be a person who carries peace
to all I see. Lord, let me be one who can
help the troubled so that they can see you
in me. Lord, I want to always be with you.

Dear God, please let me act like you. Let
the world see that I am different and then
in turn, ask me how they can be like me.
Lord, let me practice what I hear and know
you are every day to be a light in a dark
world. I love you. Amen.

<u>Revelation 2:7</u>
*He who is able to hear, let him listen to and give heed to what the Spirit says to the assemblies (churches). To him who overcomes (is victorious), I will grant to eat [of the fruit] of the tree of life, which is in the paradise of God.*

We want to be overcomers! Overcomers are those who in spite of all the odds over come in victory. That does not mean it wasn't a fight or a struggle. It doesn't mean there was not pain involved. But, it does mean we overcame and received victory.

ALL those who overcome in this world will surely be with God. This says we will be in paradise with God. This is enough motivation to keep pressing through to being called an overcomer.

Lord, help me to be an overcomer. Lord, take away doubt, fear, pain, or unbelief so that I can be called an overcomer. Lord, I know that I will spend the rest of my life with you in paradise because you helped me to be an overcomer in Christ! Amen.

Genesis 32:30
*And Jacob called the name of the place Peniel [the face of God], saying, For I have seen God face to face, and my life is spared and not snatched away.*

It was not until the last few years that I asked God to see his face. I desperately seek the contours of his face, the physical characteristics of our King. I will keep asking God until the day I meet him in Heaven to see his face.

The answer from God has been a tremendous illumination of light when I seek physically to see his face. I see great volumes of light like the rays that beam out of clouds. Pray today to see his face and see what He shows you.

Dear God, thank you that I can come to you and ask anything from you. Lord, today let us see your face in the way you would allow. Lord, we love you and we can't wait when we the day comes when we can see your face all day everyday. I love you. Amen.

<u>Exodus 3:4</u>
*And when the Lord saw that he turned aside to see, God called to him out of the midst of the bush and said, Moses, Moses! And he said, Here am I.*

What amazes me is the way that God will show up in our lives. He comes when we least expect it. God can come in any form if we just look for him.

Where is God showing up in your life? Note that Moses was looking for him. Ask God to show up in your life in a way that you know that it is God. He will answer you, but it may be in a place or time that you never thought.

Dear God, thank you that you do show up in our lives. Thank you Lord that we can look for you and that your love is so great you answer us. Lord, let my eyes see you, and help me not to overlook your presence today. I know you can show up anywhere, and all I have to do is look for you.

Deuteronomy 4:19

*And beware lest you lift up your eyes to the heavens, and when you see the sun, moon, and stars, even all the host of the heavens, you be drawn away and worship them and serve them, things which the Lord your God has allotted to all nations under the whole heaven.*

How can anyone say there is no God when you look up at a night sky, or a sunset in the late of day? There is not one sunrise, sunset, or moonstruck night that duplicates itself. Everyday there is a new splendor from God.

God made the heaven this beautiful so that the spirit man would know there is a supreme Maker called God. God made the splendor so all would know there is one true God who we are called to serve.

Dear God, thank you for the beauty of the sun, moon, and stars. The marvel leaves me speechless. Lord, you left no doubt that nothing but you could create this masterpiece. I love you. Amen

Deuteronomy 4:29
*But if from there you will seek (inquire for
and require as necessity) the Lord your
God, you will find Him if you [truly] seek
Him with all your heart [and mind] and
soul and life.*

To see God is to seek him with all that you
are. You must not give up. We must search
for God with our hearts. Tell God you love
him and to come into your heart, and you
will see him.

Tell God that you believe He is there and
real, and He will be seen in your thoughts.
Tell God in the deepest part of your soul
you seek him. He will fill you with the Holy
Spirit. Then ultimately you must surrender
your life and give it to him. Then,
 God will show all the time in many ways.

Dear God, I give you my heart, my mind,
my soul, and my life so that I may see
you in every way. Lord, thank you for
your Son, Jesus, so that we can see you
in a deep personal and intimate way.
I love you. Amen.

Deuteronomy 32:39
*See now that I, I am He, and there is no god beside Me; I kill and I make alive, I wound and I heal, and there is none who can deliver out of My hand.*

We must see in our lives that we serve NO other gods. Today we must ask ourselves, "Does anything in my life come before God?" Does my job, my wife, kids, money, or success come before what God is in my life?

God should be the first priority in our lives. He is in complete control of the world and all we do. So today, make sure that you give your priority list a run through, and give God the first slot on it.

Lord, thank you for being the one and only. Thank you that you have the power to do all things. Lord, help me today to realign my life and make you the first priority on my list. Then let my life imitate that you are first in my life! I love you. Amen.

Joshua 23:3

*And you have seen all that the Lord your God has done to all these nations for your sake; for it is the Lord your God Who has fought for you.*

What a great word today that God fights for us. This gives me so much comfort to know that for my sake, God will fight for me to win. Then I just remind myself that Jesus has paid the ultimate price by dying on the cross, shedding his blood so that death would no longer have a sting.

Many of us are in tough times. Remember God is in the ring fighting for us. Also, know that Jesus has already won it all for us by dying on Calvary's cross to give life eternal. Because of his sacrifice, we can have a deep personal relationship with God our Lord.

Dear God, thank you so much for never giving up on me. Thank you for continuing to fight on our behalf. Thank you for being my defender. I love you. Amen.

<u>2 Kings 20:5</u>
*Turn back and tell Hezekiah, the leader of My people, Thus says the Lord, the God of David your [forefather]: I have heard your prayer, I have seen your tears; behold, I will heal you. On the third day you shall go up to the house of the Lord.*

God does hear our prayers. He sees our tears. He feels our pain. Then He fills us with his grace and mercy. Healing begins.

The Lord is a God of order. He has it all planned and has a well thought out system. Cry out to him and He will make a way for you. He will heal your hurts.

Dear God, please hear my cry today. I need you to heal me today. I give you complete control to answer me in the way you want. Lord, forgive me and help me. I love you and thank you for healing me. Amen.

<u>1 Chronicles 28:8</u>
*Now therefore, in the sight of all Israel, the assembly of the Lord, and in the hearing of our God, keep and seek [to be familiar with] all the commandments of the Lord your God, that you may possess this good land and leave it as an inheritance for your children after you forever.*

We must be familiar with God. We can't just hear the word and declare we know God. We can only know him if we obey and act on his word. You can only be familiar with something that you have spent time with, or experienced personally.

We must become more familiar with who God is and what his word says. This will insure that our children and their children will be taken care of forever.

Dear God, please help me to know you in a deeper intimate way. Let me be so familiar with all you are and say. Thank you for the promise that you will leave a legacy of my relationship with you to be inherited by my grandchildren's children. I love you. Amen.

<u>2 Chronicles 15:13</u>
*And that whoever would not seek the Lord,*
*the God of Israel, should be put to death,*
*whether young or old, man or woman.*

This makes me realize the truth that God is
no respecter of person. He does not single
out male or female, rich or poor, or the
color of your skin. WE must seek the Lord.
If we don't then we will lose our life.

God is a just God. He gives us the choice
to seek and find him, and if we don't, then
we will be dead in the Lord. We must seek
God more so that we can be assured we
will live with him eternally.

Dear God, forgive me for the days that I do
not seek you. Lord, please use me to help
others find you. Lord, I want to live with
you forever. I love you. Amen.

<u>2 Chronicles 26:5</u>
*He set himself to seek God in the days of Zechariah, who instructed him in the things of God; and as long as he sought (inquired of, yearned for) the Lord, God made him prosper.*

Today we hear so many ways to prosper. There are hundreds of get rich quick schemes for sale. Greed and prosperity are everywhere. But, there is only one way to prosper.

Only by having a personal relationship with God can one prosper. He promises us that too. If we yearn to be near him and seek him then He will prosper us.

Do you want to be more prosperous today?

Dear God, please forgive me for trying to get things without you. Today Lord, I ask you to find my heart. Then Lord, I will patiently wait to live a prosperous life with you. I love you. Amen.

Ezra 8:22

*For I was ashamed to request of the king a band of soldiers and horsemen to protect us against the enemy along the way, because we had told the king, The hand of our God is upon all them for good who seek Him, but His power and His wrath are against all those who forsake Him.*

God is our supreme protection. He will use all of his power to make sure we are not defeated. I am reminded that NO devil in Hell can keep God's plan from being realized.

However, we must come to him and seek his protection. We can not forsake him or his wrath will be against us. Seek his protection no matter what war you are in and He will give you victory through HIS Power!

Dear God, the war I am in is tough. I need your protection. I seek only your divine covering and direction. Lord, use all of your powers to give me victory. I love you. Amen.

*Day 52*

<u>Job 8:5-6</u>
*⁵If you will seek God diligently and make your supplication to the Almighty, ⁶Then, if you are pure and upright, surely He will bestir Himself for you and make your righteous dwelling prosperous again.*

Supplication can be defined as a humble prayer. So again, if we diligently seek God daily, not just when we need something, and humbly pray to him often, He will restore. This behavior activates God.

God will rise to action when we come humbly with diligence. He will make all things better. Seek to stay pure and upright in your life showing God you are for real. He will answer you.

Dear God, humbly and diligently I come to you daily for help and direction. I know you will restore and give me a prosperous life. I love you. Amen

<u>Job 19:26</u>
*And after my skin, even this body, has been destroyed, then from my flesh or without it I shall see God,*

When we die, when our flesh is dead, we will see God. In the end, we will stand before God and give an account of what we have done with the lives that He gave us.

The world today makes so light of this fact. It almost tries to tell us that we may not even see God in the end. We WILL see God in front of the mercy seat, and we will give an answer to what we did here on earth.

What are you doing for God today? If you believe in Jesus, that He is the Son of the living God, you will go to heaven. But, the question is, how many are you taking with you to heaven?

Dear God, forgive me if don't share this enough so we will all stand before you. Use me to help someone see that what we do on earth matters. I love you. Amen

<u>Job 31:4</u>
*Does not [God] see my ways and count all my steps?*

Ironically, God not only counts our steps and ways but He knows the number of hairs on our head. This can be a great comfort to some. But, for some this may be a sober thought.

Don't kid yourself and think God does not see all that you do in the dark. God sees everything. Don't let the enemy deceive you on this, GOD sees it all, and everything we say or do.

Be sure to know that God knows everything about you.

Dear God, please forgive me for trying to hide things from you. You do see all that I am. Forgive my sins today and help me to make better choices. Lord, help me to do whatever you purposed for me today. I love you. Amen.

Job 33:26

*He prays to God, and He is favorable to him, so that he sees His face with joy; for [God] restores to him his righteousness (his uprightness and right standing with God - with its joys)*

Some define Joy as Jesus - First, Others - Second, and Yourself - Third. If we live our lives in this order, we will really know what JOY in Christ means.

Righteousness means right standing with God. Through the blood of Jesus, we are righteous. Nothing we do will ever make us worthy to stand before the Holy Throne. But, God will restore us into right standing with him. All we have to do is surrender and pray for forgiveness and God will restore JOY and righteousness.

Dear God, forgive my sins. Please Lord, restore my joy and my righteousness. I want to see your face of JOY in my life. I love you. Amen.

*Day 56*

<u>Job 33:28</u>
*[God] has redeemed my life from going down to the pit [of destruction], and my life shall see the light!*

What a GREAT word. God will deliver us from our own demise. He will come to us in our own self-destruction and rescue us. No matter how many the sins or what the sins are,
God will reach down into the pit to help us.

God truly loves us where we are even if we are up to our eyeballs in sin. God will restore us. God will bring us out of darkness and bring us back into the Light.

Dear God, I am drowning in my own sins. Lord, please reach from the heavens and rescue me. I need you. I need to see the light at the end of this darkness. Thank you Lord for pulling me out of the pit and self-destruction and letting me the light again! I love you. Amen.

Job 34:21
*For [God's] eyes are upon the ways of a man, and He sees all his steps.*

God really does see everything we do. Now today let's look at how we can see God. Look at the sun in the day. Look at the moon and stars at night. The majesty and splendor of his name can be seen in every angle of the earth.

Maybe we should slow down enough to admire the earth and environment God made for us to live in. Trees, flowers, grass, rain, and all of the sights to take in on a daily basis are at ours to capture by seeing God.

Dear God, today please help me to see you in a new way. Let the sun shine in a brighter way, the moon shine in a flashy way, and in all that surrounds me let my eyes acknowledge you. Let my eyes never grow weary of admiring the beauty in the nature you created for my enjoyment and pleasure.

<u>Psalm 14:2</u>
*The Lord looked down from heaven upon
the children of men to see if there were any
who understood, dealt wisely, and sought
after God, inquiring for and of Him and
requiring Him [of vital necessity].*

Are you pursuing God? Is He your vital
necessity today? It takes our action to
pursue God with passion. Pursue to know,
see, understand, hear, and feel God more
today.

Allow God today to be your vital necessity.
Let nothing else today cloud or keep
you from searching for God in every
way. Make room for God and watch him
surprise with you with filling all of your
desires.

Dear God, I search you in all my ways. Let
my actions prove to you that I diligently
seeking your will. Lord, let me see, hear,
interpret and feel you more today so that I
can be in your presence. I love you. Amen.

<u>Psalm 40:3</u>
*And He has put a new song in my mouth, a
song of praise to our God. Many shall see
and fear (revere and worship) and put their
trust and confident reliance in the Lord.*

Give God permission to rewrite your
agenda. Let him do a new thing for you in
your life and destiny. Surrender today and
ask him to touch you so that you can see
him in a new level of trust and fear.

Reverently fear his majesty, power, and
rely on him alone today. Trust God with all
of your heart with every area of your life:
career, family, marriage, finances, future,
and dreams. God will never disappoint you
and He will give you a new song for you to
sing.

Dear God, thank you for the power you
have to change the song in my mouth.
Lord, I know you are God, and I will trust
you forever. I love you. Amen.

*Day 60*

<u>Psalm 53:2</u>
*God looked down from heaven upon the children of men to see if there were any who understood, who sought (inquired after and desperately required) God.*

God wants us to desire only after him. Don't you want to be the one who God sees seeking him? God is looking for all of us to make him first today.

Try today to understand God on a deeper level. When things go wrong or hurt you, ask God what you should learn here? Dig deeper into your soul. Desperately seek God, and He will be found.

Dear God, today help me to seek only you. Let my day reflect who you are in my life by what I do hour by hour. Help me to diligently seek you for a deeper understanding of who you are.
I love you. Amen.

Psalm 69:32
*The humble shall see it and be glad; you who seek God, inquiring for and requiring Him [as your first need], let your hearts revive and live!*

Humble yourself before the Lord today. God says humble yourselves, and then He can exalt us. What a great word. Humble can be defined as not being proud or arrogant; modest. Can we really stand before God with an arrogant attitude?

How easy is it today to go before God and tell him we are completely dependent on Him? Tell God you can not do this life without Him. How easy can this be? We all are broken when we stand before Him. God promises to exalt the humble.

Dear God, I know I am a sinner. I can't do this life without you. Lord show yourself today as you exalt me out of my humbleness. Lord, thank you for always fulfilling your promises.
I love you. Amen.

<u>Psalm 70:4</u>
*May all those who seek, inquire of and for
You, and require You [as their vital need]
rejoice and be glad in You; and may those
who love Your salvation say continually,
Let God be magnified!*

God, I magnify you today. You are the
master and creator of everything. Lord, let
me see that you are vital to my life. Lord,
let me seek you in every area in my life.

Lord, you are my salvation. Let me feel the
victory of overcoming in my heart today.
Let help me to feel JOY and let me feel
like rejoicing. Let me Praise you today
over and over and feel the presence of
lightness and peace in my spirit that only
you can give.

Dear God, I praise you in every way today.
Lord, let me heart feel lighter today no
matter what comes my way. I love you.
Amen.

<u>Proverbs 11:27</u>
*He who diligently seeks good seeks [God's] favor, but he who searches after evil, it shall come upon him.*

Ask yourself today, am I drawing closer to God or farther away? Am I doing more good in my life or acting out in a sinful way?

We must seek the good in all things. Today, seek God's goodness and feel the great emotion of appreciation for him and his love for us. Pray that God's favor just overflows your spirit that all men will show you favor too.

Run from evil, or you shall live with the enemy.

Dear God, thank you for showing me favor for seeking the good and seeking the goodness of you. Lord, deliver me from my evil ways so that I can live in you favor. If I have favor with God then man will favor me too. I love you. Amen.

Isaiah 41:17

*The poor and needy are seeking water when there is none; their tongues are parched with thirst. I the Lord will answer them; I, the God of Israel, will not forsake them.*

This scripture should give you so much comfort. Here God says that we will never be thirsty. God will always answer our needs. The Lord is so compassionate to the needy and the poor.

God's love will never leave us. God will never forsake us. Nothing will stand in the way of God's love for us. Ask God to comfort you in such a way today that He is with you always no matter how bad things may seem.

Lord, thank you that I will never be thirsty. Lord, thank you loving me always and for never leaving me. Lord, thank you for you compassion for the poor and needy and for offering comfort that only you can give. I love you. Amen.

<u>Isaiah 44:18</u>
*They do not know or understand, for their eyes God has let become besmeared so that they cannot see, and their minds as well so that they cannot understand.*

Besmear can be defined as defile. That means that many were polluting who you are. Lord, please today do not blind my eyes to who you are.

Lord, open up my mind today so that I have new insight to the word in a new way. Lord, let me feel you today by seeing you and expanding the limits of what you are in my mind.

Dear God, let me never go blind to who you are. Let my life never defile who you are. Let my mind comprehend the word in a deeper place in my heart. Lord, thank you for keeping my eyes open and my mind alert to who you are today. I love you. Amen.

<u>Lamentations 3:25</u>
*The Lord is good to those who wait
hopefully and expectantly for Him, to those
who seek Him [inquire of and for Him and
require Him by right of necessity and on
the authority of God's word].*

Don't we all want God to be good to us?
Our answer to that is right here today.
God says those who wait with HOPE and
expectancy will be treated well by the
Lord. Ask God today to stand firm on his
promises for your life.

God loves for us to remind him of what
He has already said will come to pass. You
must do your part and speak it, then God
promises at due season He will bring it to
pass.

Dear God, help me to wait on you
patiently. Lord, I find hope in you. Lord,
I expect you to fulfill all of your promises
for my life. I love you. Amen.

<u>Daniel 2:47</u>
*The king answered Daniel, Of a truth your God is the God of gods and the Lord of kings and a revealer of secret mysteries, seeing that you could reveal this secret mystery!*

God, thank you for giving us the secret desires of our hearts. Thank you for never failing us. God will not fail us or release his hold on us. God, you will reveal the mysteries to me.

Today Lord, reveal to me a new way to see you. Lord, you said we would get the deepest secret desire of out hearts. Lord, do that today so that I feel you in a new way.

Dear God, I know you do what you say. Lord, you will reveal the mysteries of who you are. Lord, thank you for giving me the desires of my heart. I love you. Amen

<u>Zechariah 9:14</u>
*And the Lord shall be seen over them and His arrow shall go forth as the lightning, and the Lord God will blow the trumpet and will go forth in the windstorms of the south.*

Today we see that God can come as lightning.
The Lord can be heard as a trumpet or show up as a windstorm. What an incredible hope.

God can manifest himself in any way. Joy comes to the weeping. Burning bushes that speak God's words. Lord, today, will you show me and allow me to see you in a physical manifestation? Let me hear you in an extraordinary way that I know it is you.

Lord, let me feel your presence today by seeing you in a physical way or hearing you in supernatural way. Lord, thank you that you can come to me in any way that you choose best for me. I love you. Amen.

<u>Matthew 5:8</u>
*Blessed (happy, enviably fortunate, and spiritually prosperous - possessing the happiness produced by the experience of God's favor and especially conditioned by the revelation of His grace, regardless of their outward conditions) are the pure in heart, for they shall see God!*

How exciting! To day we will feel the happiness of God! We declare today that God will bless, prosper, favor, and give us happiness because we long to see God.

It's a discipline of the mind to stay focused on all the good things God has promised us. So, today, make this a habit for you. Tell God all of the things He has promised us for keeping our hearts pure and our intentions all about him.

God, thank you for giving me happiness, fortune, favor, and grace today. Help me to everyday declare all the good things you are and good things you promise for me. I love you Amen.

Matthew 13:17
*Truly I tell you, many prophets and righteous men [men who were upright and in right standing with God] yearned to see what you see, and did not see it, and to hear what you hear, and did not hear it.*

This proves to me that many will live on earth without a glimpse of who God is. Even though Jesus came so that we all have the opportunity to see God, many will not. We are so blessed today that when we read these words we personally know who inspired them.

Today we need to reach out to an unbeliever in our life. We need to help them see God and bring them in the light of knowledge. It's so easy to do this. Just tell them God loves them and ask them if they will study with you. They can see who God is as you reveal who He is in your life.

Dear God, help me to know who I need to reach out to. Lord, let me hear your voice as you instruct me on how to save my loved one. I love you. Amen.

<u>Luke 3:6</u>
*And all mankind shall see (behold and understand and at last acknowledge) the salvation of God (the deliverance from eternal death decreed by God).*

It is great to know that ALL of us will see the God of all creation. He alone has delivered us from death through salvation. He gave us his only Son to die on the Cross and shed his blood obedient to death.

Have you received deliverance from God? Is there anything that keeps you from seeing and understanding who God is? If yes, fall to your knees and ask God to break the chains that bind you from living a life eternally in heaven.

Dear God, please deliver me from anything that stands in the way of feeling and knowing your presence. I want to live forever with you. Thank you for allowing Jesus to die on the cross to become my Savior. I love you. Amen.

<u>Luke 6:21</u>
*Blessed (happy-- with life-joy and satisfaction in God's favor and salvation, apart from your outward condition - and to be envied) are you who hunger and seek with eager desire now, for you shall be filled and completely satisfied!*

Do you seek happiness? Do you feel happy? Do you have favor from God? Do you have a joyful heart?

In order to feel the JOY of Christ we must die to the outward man. We must seek the deep parts of our spirit and desire a more intimate relationship with God. Then, you will feel JOY, happiness, and feel favor from the Lord.

Dear God, thank you for giving me Joy. Thank you that you bless me with happiness when I seek only you. Lord, help me not to fall into the world's draw and help my heart to seek only you.

<u>Luke 17:15</u>
*Then one of them, upon seeing that he
was cured, turned back, recognizing and
thanking and praising God with a loud
voice;*

Oh, how God loves to be thanked! God
cures us all the time. DO we acknowledge
a broken heart healed, a sickness that
subsides, and a relationship rekindled?

In order to feel the overflow of God's
presence today come to him with a
thankful heart. Today make a list for God
that tells him all of the things for which
you are so thankful. God will surely smile
upon you for this heart of thanks.

Dear God, forgive me for not praising you
more. Lord, help me to thank you more for
the things you do for me all the time. Lord,
I thank you for all that you do for me. I
love you. Amen.

Luke 17:21

*Nor will people say, Look! Here [it is]! or,
See, [it is] there! For behold, the kingdom
of God is within you [in your hearts] and
among you [surrounding you].*

What I find amazing here is the fact that
God's kingdom resides within us. So much
of our time is spent looking on the outside
for God. God's spirit lives within us.

Today, pray to the spirit inside of you and
ask that you see a power you have never
seen. Ask the Lord to show you something
about yourself that is not a natural
characteristic but a characteristic of who
God is in you.

Lord, show me today a trait of who you
are inside of me. Show me who I might
touch by acting out in your spirit and not
in my flesh. Lord, help me to do this more
everyday so that others will see more of
your character than my flesh. I love you.
Amen.

<u>John 1:18</u>
*No man has ever seen God at any time;*
*the only unique Son, or the only begotten*
*God, Who is in the bosom [in the intimate*
*presence] of the Father, He has declared*
*Him [He has revealed Him and brought*
*Him out where He can be seen; He has*
*interpreted Him and He has made Him*
*known].*

The intimate presence of God is seen
through his only Son, Jesus. All of the kind
acts and compassion are what God is to us.
The Lord offers all of this to us.

Ask God to show compassion to you today.
Ask the Lord to touch your heart and
reveal Jesus in a new way to you. Look
for what Jesus represents and how He acts,
and you will see who God is and how his
presence can be seen.

Dear God, thank you for your compassion.
Thank you for your love. Thank you that
we have Jesus through whom you reveal
who you are. I love you. Amen.

<u>John 1:51</u>
*Then He said to him, I assure you, most solemnly I tell you all, you shall see heaven opened, and the angels of God ascending and descending upon the Son of Man!*

Do you believe in angels? Angels are mentioned all through the Bible. You really do have angels of protection around you. One day as this scripture states, we will see them with Jesus.

If you need help in believing in the existence in angels, ask God today to show you his angels. Ask God to bring the angels to your rescue. God will always deliver to you in his perfect timing.

Lord, thank you that you have helpers called angels. Thank you for the protection you give me. Lord, rescue me today through the sight of your angels. I love you. Amen.

<u>John 3:3</u>
*Jesus answered him, I assure you, most
solemnly I tell you, that unless a person is
born again (anew, from above), he cannot
ever see (know, be acquainted with, and
experience) the kingdom of God.*

Have you been born again? Have you
asked Jesus into your heart to be your
Savior? Have you confessed that Jesus is
the Son of God and that He died for your
sins? Have you been baptized like Jesus
was baptized in the Jordan River?

Today, if you have never asked Jesus into
your heart as the Lord of your life, do it.
If you have confessed and have been born
again, ask for a deeper relationship with
God today.

Dear God, thank you for your only Son
dying for me on a cross. I want to make
you the Lord of my life. Lord, I want and
desire a deeper relationship with you. Lord,
touch me today and bring me closer to your
heart. I love you. Amen.

<u>Acts 2:17</u>
*And it shall come to pass in the last days,
God declares, that I will pour out of My
Spirit upon all mankind, and your sons
and your daughters shall prophesy [telling
forth the divine counsels] and your young
men shall see visions (divinely granted
appearances), and your old men shall
dream [divinely suggested] dreams.*

We are in the last days. Personally, I see
every one of these events occurring today.
My own daughter at age fifteen is seeing
prophetic dreams and visions.

Do you know where you will go if Jesus
comes before today's end? Are you living
as if today may be your last? Do you
want to spend the rest of your existence in
heaven or hell?

Dear God, I want to be with you forever.
You said that if we believe in you and that
your Son Jesus came to set us free, then
I would spend eternity with you. Lord, I
declare that today. I can't wait to see you in
Heaven. I love you. Amen

<u>Acts 10:40</u>
*But God raised Him to life on the third day and caused Him to be manifest (to be plainly seen),*

Isn't this incredible? God raised Jesus from the dead and made him visible to many! Can you imagine the faces when they saw Jesus alive after they had watched in agony as He died on the cross?

I love Simon Peter's response; he asked to see the holes in his palm from the nails they drove in when He was put on the cross. I love the fact Peter was like most of us - he needed proof that it was for real. The absolute truth is that Jesus proved that it was he. God actually raised him from the dead.

Dear God, thank you for always answering the questions we have before we even ask them. Thank you for Jesus. I love you. Amen.

*Day 80*

<u>Acts 17:27</u>
*So that they should seek God, in the hope that they might feel after Him and find Him, although He is not far from each one of us.*

The answer to all of life is in this scripture. We must seek God every second of every day. Seek his knowledge. Seek his will for us. Seek his directions. Seek his character. Seek his approval. Seek his Holiness. Seek the righteousness of him.

God is NOT far from any of us. God waits for us to come to him. He gives us free choice. Are you seeking him in very area of your life? Are you seeking heavenward or are you stuck with the world is telling you?

God, thank you for being right here with us. Lord, you will direct our entire life if we seek you. Lord, thank you for never leaving us. Help me to seek you on a deeper level today. I love you. Amen.

<u>Romans 11:8</u>

*As it is written, God gave them a spirit (an attitude) of stupor, eyes that should not see and ears that should not hear, [that has continued] down to this very day.*

The Lord will keep you from seeing him. God can keep you from hearing him. He continues today to keep eyes and ears shut. He does this so that you will get desperate enough to find him.

It's amazing what we believe when we get desperate enough. Many who don't believe in healing come to God for healing as soon as they are diagnosed with cancer. Don't wait to get in a desperate situation to see and hear God.

Dear God, please allow me to see and hear you always. Don't let me ever have a spirit that can't see or hear. Lord, I love you. Amen.

*Day 82*

<u>1 Corinthians 2:9</u>
*What eye has not seen and ear has not heard and has not entered into the heart of man, [all that] God has prepared (made and keeps ready) for those who love Him*

I am a living testimony for this scripture. God has given me a life that I could not have even dreamed. He has taken care of every area of my life in such a way my eyes had never dreamed to see or my ears to hear. God has touched my heart in such a way that now I live every second of every day for him.

Don't ever give up on what God can do for you. I dared to believe, and God matched that faith. God gave me a life I could never have imagined. God will go to all lengths for those who Love him

Lord, thank you that you have prepared the best for those who love you. You are an amazing God. Lord, help me to keep my beliefs strong so that you can meet my faith with the super naturalness of you. I love you. Amen

<u>1 Corinthians 13:12</u>
*For now we are looking in a mirror that gives only a dim (blurred) reflection [of reality as in a riddle or enigma], but then [when perfection comes] we shall see in reality and face to face! Now I know in part (imperfectly), but then I shall know and understand fully and clearly, even in the same manner as I have been fully and clearly known and understood [by God].*

God asks us to look in the mirror. What do you see when you look in the mirror? I tell many when you are making a very important decision to make sure that you can look yourself in the mirror.

God sees you through the blood of Christ. We are in right standing with God because of Jesus. Now, look at yourself through the blood too!

Dear God, help me to use the mirror to make the choices you approve of. Lord, thank you for Jesus' blood. I love you. Amen.

2 Corinthians 4:4
*For the god of this world has blinded the unbelievers' minds [that they should not discern the truth], preventing them from seeing the illuminating light of the Gospel of the glory of Christ (the Messiah), Who is the Image and Likeness of God.*

A great definition of a "god" that I use is anything that you put before God becomes your "god." What is on the top of your priority list? What is the top slot of your to-do list? What does your checkbook ledger look like? If you place those things before God, you are making them your "gods."

The gods of this world, the darkness and perversion, will blind you. You will lie in eternal darkness. If you don't seek Jesus, you will stay in the dark. Look for Jesus in every way and everyday and act it out in you daily life. Then you will see who God is.

Dear God, help me to make you the top of all my lists. Lord, help me to make you first in everything. I love you. Amen.

<u>Galatians 1:10</u>
*Now am I trying to win the favor of men, or of God? Do I seek to please men? If I were still seeking popularity with men, I should not be a bond servant of Christ (the Messiah).*

The bottom line or the big question to ask is, "Am I living for God's approval, or am I living for man's approval?" That is it in a nut shell. I ask myself often what it will gain me to gain the whole world but MISS God.

Don't miss God today. Feel his touch, hear his word, and see him in your life. God is all around. Make a commitment today to live for God's approval, not man's. God says He looks only at the heart. Is your heart genuinely set on pleasing him?

Lord, help me to focus on just YOU. Lord, forgive me again for getting caught in the world's definition of what success is and who I should be. Lord, I want only to please you today. I love you. Amen.

<u>Philippians 2:15</u>

*That you may show yourselves to be blameless and guiltless, innocent and uncontaminated, children of God without blemish (faultless, unrebukable) in the midst of a crooked and wicked generation [spiritually perverted and perverse], among whom you are seen as bright lights (stars or beacons shining out clearly) in the [dark] world,*

Lord, I know I can never be blameless. But I do want more than anything to be a light of hope in this dark world. Lord, I thank you for the ability to stand before you in the righteousness of Christ.

Lord, we do live in a perverse sick world. Use me as a bright shining star to touch someone who needs you. Lord, help me to show someone a better way and to see things clearer.

Lord, thank you for the blood of Christ. Thank you for knowing how dark this world is. Lord, thank you for your Son the Light of the world. I love you. Amen.

Philippians 4:9

*Practice what you have learned and
received and heard and seen in me, and
model your way of living on it, and the God
of peace (of untroubled, undisturbed well-
being) will be with you.*

This scripture clearly shows it takes
practice to do what is right. Our human
nature defies the Spirit to do the right thing.
As a follower of Christ we must practice
daily the words Jesus gave us to be like
him.

Today ask God to make you stronger in
your walk. Exercise patience, generosity,
but most importantly LOVE today. We
must model our lives after God's own Son
so we can live in peace. Feel God's peace
today as you model after Christ.

Dear God, thank you for sending a perfect
model for us to emulate. Lord, I want to
feel your peace today. Lord, help me to
practice daily what Jesus told us to do and
to love people deeper today. Thank you,
Lord. I love you. Amen.

<u>Colossians 3:1</u>
*If then you have been raised with Christ [to a new life, thus sharing His resurrection from the dead], aim at and seek the [rich, eternal treasures] that are above, where Christ is, seated at the right hand of God.*

This really hit home today for me because this week in ministry has been a challenge. I have had to tell myself often that what I am doing down here is building treasures in heaven. This keeps me motivated not to quit.

How about you? Are your eyes and activities pointing towards heaven? Are you living for God today or the world? Are you seeking the rich eternal treasures in heaven as a new creation in Christ? If not, start today.

Dear God, please help me not to give up. Please help me to keep my eyes on you and the treasures I am laying up in heaven. Keep me from getting caught up in the world today and getting discouraged. Let me live in victory today. I love you. Amen

<u>1 Timothy 3:16</u>
And great and important and weighty, we *confess, is the hidden truth (the mystic secret) of godliness. He [God] was made visible in human flesh, justified and vindicated in the [Holy] Spirit, was seen by angels, preached among the nations, believed on in the world, [and] taken up in glory.*

God is a mystery. He loves to use this definition for himself. However, He promises us that in Jesus Christ the mysteries will be revealed.

We must look in our Spirits to solve the mysteries of God. God will reveal the power and knowledge and make visible to us what He desires for us to know. Ask him today to reveal a mystery for your own needs today, and He will be present in your day.

Dear God, help me to see you and hear you with my Spirit. Reveal the mysteries you need me to know for my own personal life today. I love you. Amen.

<u>1 John 3:17</u>
*But if anyone has this world's goods
(resources for sustaining life) and sees his
brother and fellow believer in need, yet
closes his heart of compassion against him,
how can the love of God live and remain in
him?*

Whoa! I love this scripture! Many of us find
success on so many levels in this life. Many
have money, successful careers, and all kinds
of material blessings. YET, when someone is
in obvious need, we turn our back.

Ask the Lord to use you today to be his
vessel. Allow God to nudge and touch you
today to show you who really needs a gift
from you. It could be a lunch date, a raise, or
just a monetary gift for a happy. You will be
amazed at the response and how much God
will bless you in return for being a vessel
that gives.

Dear God, show me today who needs a gift.
Lord, help me to be a better giver and to
listen more to you. Thank you for all of my
blessings. I love you. Amen.

<u>1 John 4:12</u>
*No man has at any time [yet] seen God.*
*But if we love one another, God abides*
*(lives and remains) in us and His love (that*
*love which is essentially His) is brought to*
*completion (to its full maturity, runs its full*
*course, is perfected) in us!*

Oh God, we can't wait to see you. What a day that will be when we know that we have a final resting place with you. Lord, sometimes it is so hard feeling you in this crazy world. Lord, let me love others so I can one day be in the presence of your love forever.

Lord, I want to feel you today as I abide in you. As I strive today to stay closely connected in what you say and tell me to do. Lord let me love on a whole new level so that I can be perfected through you.

Lord, let me feel your love today. Then, help me to love others so that your love can be perfected through me. Thank you for loving me. I love you. Amen

<u>Numbers 14:22</u>
*Because all those men who have seen My glory and My [miraculous] signs which I performed in Egypt and in the wilderness, yet have tested and proved Me these ten times and have not heeded My voice.*

God is still making miraculous moves today! You don't have to look far. People are getting well from terrible illnesses. Marriages are completely restored. Shaky finances are being replaced with prosperity. But we must believe.

Do you believe God is still performing miracles today? By the measure you believe is the measure of result you will receive. Look around. Ask some spiritual friend. I am sure you will hear a story today of his miraculous wonders.

Dear God, help me with my measure of belief in your ability to perform miracles. Lord, I know you are the God who does the impossible, and today I ask you to do this for me so that I can feel your presence of victory.

<u>Matthew 24:30</u>
*Then the sign of the Son of Man will
appear in the sky, and then all the tribes of
the earth will mourn and beat their breasts
and lament in anguish, and they will see
the Son of Man coming on the clouds of
heaven with power and great glory [in
brilliancy and splendor].*

We will see Jesus coming. Jesus is coming
back to judge the end of the world. Jesus
will appear in the clouds in brilliance. Are
you ready?

Have you taken Jesus as your personal
Savior? Do you make him Lord of your
life? If you have not, then today when you
pray this prayer, pray with your whole
heart, and you will never be the same
again.

Dear Jesus, I take you into my heart today.
I declare that you are the Son of God who
died on the cross and shed your blood for
my sins. God, today I make you the Lord
of my life. Thank you for your Son and the
eternal life you give me today.

<u>John 5:44</u>
*How is it possible for you to believe [how can you learn to believe], you who [are content to seek and] receive praise and honor and glory from one another, and yet do not seek the praise and honor and glory which come from Him who alone is God?*

Sometimes God will allow us to wallow in our unbelief. God will let us live in the sin we have created. The only way to get out of this is to seek praise from God alone.

Let us not grow content with what the world tells us is "Making it." Jesus said He came to give us a life of abundance! Are you living in abundance? Seek God's praise alone, honor him with your life, and give God all the glory of your life. He will bless you abundantly.

Lord, you said I can live life of abundance. Today Lord, help me to raise my expectations of what you have in store for me. Let me feel you through a new sense of confidence. I love you. Amen.

<u>John 7:18</u>

*He who speaks on his own authority
seeks to win honor for himself. [He whose
teaching originates with himself seeks
his own glory.] But He Who seeks the
glory and is eager for the honor of Him
Who sent Him, He is true; and there is no
unrighteousness or falsehood or deception
in Him.*

Are we speaking God's words daily? Are
we claiming authority over the enemy on
earth? Are we seeking the approval and
honor from man?

God wants us to seek him with pure
intentions. God knows our hearts, and He
knows who is trying to seek glory for his
own reward. We cannot deceive God. Ask
yourself "Am I speaking God's words and
seeking His approval or the world's?"

Dear God, help me to speak your truth in
my words. Lord, I desire only to honor you.
Forgive me for trying to gain the world's
approval. Touch me today as you give me a
glimpse of your glory and honor. Amen.

<u>Romans 2:7</u>
*To those who by patient persistence in well-doing [springing from piety] seek [unseen but sure] glory and honor and [ the eternal blessedness of] immortality, He will give eternal life.*

This really resonates with me today. I am practicing persistence like never before. Many days I feel I just can't make it to the finish line. I lay my head down on my pillow some days in a desperate state of exhaustion.

God can touch all of us today as we persistently pursue his goals for our lives. He will honor our diligence, particularly when it cost us. Feel God today as we lay our exhausted minds and body at the cross, and give God the opportunity to give us a spring in our step.

Lord, thank you for lifting us up when we are tired. Lord, help us to be more patient and persistent in our walk with you. Thank you for seeing it all in our lives and giving us hope of living forever with you. I love you. Amen.

<u>Deuteronomy 4:19</u>
*And beware lest you lift up your eyes to the heavens, and when you see the sun, moon, and stars, even all the host of the heavens, you be drawn away and worship them and serve them, things which the Lord your God has allotted to all nations under the whole heaven.*

This reminds me to not allow anything to replace the number one spot on my priority list. Past generations worshiped the sun, stars, and moon. Presently, we worship things and standards the world offers.

What are you worshipping today - a promotion, a raise, a new car, what the world tells you is valuable? Make sure you put God at the top of your to do list, worship him alone, and reject the world today!

Dear God, please forgive me for letting you slip out of the top slot on my to-do list. Lord, I place you first today, and I know I will feel your presence draw close to me as you promised. I love you. Amen.

<u>Psalm 23:4</u>
*Yes, though I walk through the [deep, sunless] valley of the shadow of death, I will fear or dread no evil, for You are with me; Your rod [to protect] and Your staff [to guide], they comfort me.*

Oh Father, today I will feel your presence because I ask you to keep me in the light. Lord, I lay down all of my fears today at the feet of Jesus. Lord, I know I have eternal life with you, and I remind myself today that I will never have to fear death.

Lord, thank you for allowing me to feel you today as the fear and dread break off of my heart. You say that no weapon formed against me shall prosper, and I praise you for that today!

Lord, today I declare you are the Light! No longer will I fear death. You will keep me from evil, and you will protect me and guide me today. Thank you for the peace I feel today. I love you. Amen.

Psalm 84:11

*For the Lord God is a Sun and Shield; the
Lord bestows [present] grace and favor
and [future] glory (honor, splendor, and
heavenly bliss)! No good thing will He
withhold from those who walk uprightly.*

God will never keep an answered prayer or
blessing from you! He is our shield. He is
our present grace and favor. If we will just
walk in his ways and in alignment to what
He has asked us to do.

God will touch you today as you look upon
him as your shield and sun. Close your
eyes under the sun and feel the warmth of
the rays. Now allow this warmth to filtrate
your heart and there God's touch is felt.
This manifestation will make walking
upright easy!

Dear God, touch me with the warmth of the
sun's rays from the outside in. Help me to
keep my steps today be the ones you have
ordered. Thank you for your favor and
grace. I love you. Amen.

*Day 100*

Psalm 104:19

*[The Lord] appointed the moon for the seasons; the sun knows [the exact time of] its setting.*

Again I feel such comfort in knowing God created the Seasons. God is a God of order. He knows exactly what is going to happen.

Do you have the faith and trust in God that He knows every detail of your life? He even knows when the sun is setting daily. He never forgets his own. God knows exactly what will happen.

Lord, today let me feel you in my day to day by acknowledging you are an exact God. You know exactly who I am, exactly the time of day, and exactly when time will end. I love you. Thank you for being a God of exactness. I love you. Amen.

<u>Jeremiah 31:35</u>
*Thus says the Lord, Who gives the sun for a light by day and the fixed order of the moon and of the stars for a light by night, Who stirs up the sea's roaring billows or stills the waves when they roar - the Lord of hosts is His name:*

Isn't it comforting today to know that God ordered all of the creation? God knew just where to put the moon. He knew where the stars of night would remain. It is amazing that He controls the rolls of the seas in the waves.

Do you allow him to control your steps? Do you acknowledge that God has your best interest at heart? Receive the peace that comes with the knowledge that He truly is in control of all areas of your life.

Dear God, please forgive me for trying to control everything. Lord, I allow you to control my day today. Lord, let me feel you today by peace overflowing my heart knowing you are the God who controls it all.

<u>Joel 2:31</u>
*The sun shall be turned to darkness and the moon to blood before the great and terrible day of the Lord comes.*

Today I felt such a tremble in my spirit because God is coming back. No matter what the media and modern day thinking tells us, God is coming to judge us all. The scary details of even the sun going dark bring fear to my spirit.

Our eyes will see the darkness and the moon turning to blood. Today ask God to show your eyes the light of Christ. Allow God to erase the fear of death and judgment by touching your heart. Let God assure you to whom you belong. You are God's child.

Thank you Lord, that I will not have to die and live eternally in darkens. Let me feel your touch as a Father so I will know that I am yours today. I love you. Amen.

Habakkuk 3:4

*And His brightness was like the sunlight; rays streamed from His hand, and there [in the sun like splendor] was the hiding place of His power.*

Amazing that God's splendor will be seen like the sun! Sun rays will actually come from his hand. All of this grand and bright light is the holding place of all of God's power.

Call upon God's power to touch you today. Ask the Lord to give you something that has been hidden for some time. Search your heart and ask the power of God to answer that deepest prayer you have on your heart. God will answer you!

Dear God, you are awesome. I can't wait to be blinded by your light and power. Today Lord, touch me by answering the deepest prayer of my heart that I reveal to you. I love you. Amen.

Matthew 13:43
*Then will the righteous (those who are upright and in right standing with God) shine forth like the sun in the kingdom of their Father. Let him who has ears [to hear] be listening, and let him consider and perceive and understand by hearing.*

Lord, I long to be the source of light of you. Lord, let your Spirit shine through my life, my thoughts, and my actions. Today, Lord, let others see that there is truly something different in me than the world has to offer.

Lord, let me radiate the Love of Christ to someone who least expects it today. Then, I will be able to see you today when I act through what you shine through me to someone else.

Dear Father, Let me seek to be your light in this very dark world. Let the light be a characteristic that sets me apart and a light that gives only you the glory. I love you. Amen.

Matthew 17:2

*And His appearance underwent a change in their presence; and His face shone clear and bright like the sun, and His clothing became as white as light.*

Lord, let us long today to see you face to face. Let us live in the hope that we will one day watch your face change right before our eyes. Lord, please clothe us in your light today.

Lord, let me share the hope to all I see today that we will one day see you as bright as the sun. Lord, let us feel you today by the spirit of encouragement you will place in my heart.

Lord, use me to be a mouthpiece of hope today. Help me to tell someone that heaven is a real place. Help me to share that one day you will stand face to face with all of us as bright as the sun. I love you. Amen.

Matthew 24:29

*Immediately, after the tribulation of those days the sun will be darkened, and the moon will not shed its light, and the stars will fall from the sky, and the powers of the heavens will be shaken.*

There is coming a day where all things on earth will end. Most importantly, God is returning! Jesus is coming back. Are you ready? Are you ready to see the sun go dark, watch the stars fall out of the sky, and feel the earth shake?

The path of the righteous grows brighter and brighter. Make sure that you are ready right this second to soar into the heavens with Jesus. Don't kid yourself or put off what you know what is right because today may be your last.

Lord, I know you are coming back. Lord, help me to live as if this day is my last. Lord, I long to live with you in heaven forever. I hope to see your great power today. I love you. Amen.

<u>Acts 26:13</u>
*When on the road at midday, O king, I saw a light from heaven surpassing the brightness of the sun, flashing about me and those who were traveling with me.*

God will take drastic measures in order for you to see him! He will allow you to get so low that the only place to turn is to him! Don't wait until God has to really shake you down or blind you too.

Make choices today that reflect to God you are reaching for him. Show God by taking little steps daily to draw closer to him and what He desires for us to do.

Dear God, I want to be more like you. I don't want you to have let me go so low that you have to take desperate measures to get me to turn my life around. Help me to draw closer to you. I love you. Amen.

<u>1 Corinthians 15:40</u>
*There are heavenly bodies (sun, moon, and stars) and there are earthly bodies (men, animals, and plants), but the beauty and glory of the heavenly bodies is of one kind, while the beauty and glory of earthly bodies is a different kind.*

This is such a cool concept and description of what we will look like when we get to heaven. It's all right here. Our heavenly bodies will be illuminated. They will not be like our earthly bodies. We all will be described as beautiful and glorious when we make it to heaven.

Sometimes we get so caught up in what our earthly bodies look like. Some of us are sick, and we don't want to get to heaven in that state. But, it states right here we will all have glorious and beautiful heavenly bodies.

Dear God, thank you that we will not have our aging and sick earthly bodies forever. Thank you for giving us your glory when we get to heaven I love you. Amen.

1 Corinthians 15:41

*The sun is glorious in one way, the moon is glorious in another way, and the stars are glorious in their own [distinctive] way; for one star differs from and surpasses another in its beauty and brilliance.*

What an incredible analogy. We are all glorious in our own way. We all have a distinctive purpose. Although we may all look the same, we all are distinctively different.

Look in the sky. Don't many of the stars look exactly alike? But, they are at a much closer look, very distinctively different. We all have a specific purpose which no one else can fulfill down here but you!

Dear God, thank you for giving us all a unique purpose. Lord, help me to do what ever you have called me to do on earth. Let me see that I am gloriously made with a distinctive gift designed to bring you glory. I love you. Amen.

Revelation 1:16

*In His right hand He held seven stars, and
from His mouth there came forth a sharp
two-edged sword, and His face was like the
sun shining in full power at midday.*

This is a description of what our glorious
King will appear like. All of the scriptures
describe the light of his face and presence
as a brilliant light. Here we see that his
presence is like the sun shining full power
at noon, at its strongest.

Ask God to shine his face upon you. Ask
him that his glory fall upon you. Then all
men will know that you are his.

Dear God, let my life illuminate all the
great things you are. Lord, use me as a
light in this dark world to bring you glory.
Lord, shine your face and glory upon me
today. I love you. Amen.

<u>Revelation 21:23</u>
*And the city has no need of the sun nor of
the moon to give light to it, for the splendor
and radiance (glory) of God illuminate it,
and the Lamb is its lamp.*


Can you imagine not needing a lamp? Can
you imagine no need for lights anywhere?
Turn off all your lights right now or when
it is night and see how dark it truly is.

The Lord will illuminate the heavens in
such a way there will be no need for lights
anywhere. No need for lamps. No need
for street lights. God will light the entire
world.

Thank you, Lord, for giving us such great
descriptions of your appearance. Lord, we
know you will shine so bright that there
will be no need for any more light. Lord,
thank you for crating heaven so that we
may one day see the light of your glory. I
love you. Amen.

<u>Revelation 22:5</u>
*And there shall be no more night; they have no need for lamp light or sunlight, for the Lord God will illuminate them and be their light, and they shall reign [as kings] forever and ever (through the eternities of the eternities)*

Here we see that not only is there no need for light because of God's brightness, but we shall illuminate in light too. We will illuminate light through him. We too shall reign as Kings for all eternity.

Isn't this information worth us keeping our eyes heavenward? Don't you want o live in the physical light of God? Don't you want to live as a King forever? Then, give God your all today.

Dear God, thank you for heaven. Thank you for making us so much like you. Lord, I long to come to heaven with you forever. I love you. Amen.

<u>Revelation 21:11</u>
*Clothed in God's glory [in all its splendor and radiance]. The luster of it resembled a rare and most precious jewel, like jasper, shining clear as crystal.*

This excites me so that God loves fine stones of beauty. I can only imagine what heaven must look like. God loves fine things. God loves beautiful colors. The marvel we must experience when we see the glory of what God has prepared for us.

The radiance of God's glory will be more than our eyes can conceive. Everything in heaven will be glorious and rare. God has left nothing out when it comes to the splendor of heaven.

Lord, we long to see the beauty you have created in heaven. Lord, thank you for taking such great lengths to create the splendor. I love you. Amen.

<u>1 John 3:20</u>
*Whenever our hearts in [tormenting] self-accusation make us feel guilty and condemn us. [For we are in God's hands.] For He is above and greater than our consciences (our hearts), and He knows (perceives and understands) everything [nothing is hidden from Him].*

Oh how the enemy loves to make us beat ourselves up. The enemy constantly tries to remind us of all of our terrible sins. Satan tries to keep us in self condemnation so that we will keep away from God.

Today go to God, ask for complete forgiveness through the blood of Christ, and ask him to release you from any guilt and shame. God will not only forgive you of ALL of your sins but He even forgets.

Dear God, forgive me for failing you. Please forgive me for all of my sins. Jesus, please cover me with the blood of the cross. Thank you, God, not only for forgiving me but also for forgetting my sins. I love you Amen.

<u>1 John 3:21</u>
*And, beloved, if our consciences (our hearts) do not accuse us [if they do not make us feel guilty and condemn us], we have confidence (complete assurance and boldness) before God,*

Sometimes I just need to be reminded that God forgives. Many days when I fail, I forget God is waiting for me to repent, ready to forgive. It's nice to see that God does not sit in heaven making a tally of all of my mistakes.

Boldly go before God today and ask him to give you the confidence of Forgiveness. God will touch your heart so that your shame will melt away. God is not the accuser. Satan is the accuser. God just waits patiently for us to ask for forgiveness, and then, more than willing, He does.

Dear God, thank you for your forgiveness. Thank you that you don't keep a running tally of my faults, I love you. Amen.

<u>Genesis 6:6</u>
*And the Lord regretted that He had made man on the earth, and He was grieved at heart.*

This is one of the most powerful scriptures for me. God was grieved at heart. God was so sad for man. The grief was so bad that He regretted even making man on earth!

This shows me the level of Love God has for us! It absolutely pains God to such a level when all breaks loose on earth. God truly grieves for us.

Feel God's grief and empathy for you today in your pain, disappointment, and hurts. God did not design earth to be painful. Feel God's touch as you hear his heart break right besides yours.

Dear God, thank you for grieving me so that I know I am not alone in my pain. Thank you for trying to make this world a better place by sending us your Son, Jesus. I love you. Amen.

Exodus 7:3
*And I will make Pharaoh's heart stubborn and hard, and multiply My signs, My wonders, and miracles in the land of Egypt.*
Exodus 7:2-4 *(in Context)* Exodus 7 *(Whole Chapter)*
Exodus 7:13
*But Pharaoh's heart was hardened and stubborn and he would not listen to them, just as the Lord had said.*

I used these scriptures today to show you that God deals only with our hearts. God will not allow us to deny him forever.

Does your life show the world that you believe in God's supernatural powers and miracles? Are you denying God by the way you live?

Be careful. God will harden hearts to those who do not listen to him.

Dear God, help my life to show the world who you are! Make my heart pliable to all of your ways. I love you. Amen.

Exodus 36:2

*And Moses called Bezalel and Aholiab and every able and wise hearted man in whose mind the Lord had put wisdom and ability, everyone whose heart stirred him up to come to do the work;*

What has God stirred your heart to do? Some of you may be asking, "How do I know what God wants me to do?" I tell people all the time, God tells us something or places something on our hearts, and it will not go away.

Have you ever felt the need to call someone and don't know why? Then a few days later when you still haven't called them, you still have it on your heart to do so? That's God stirring you to do it!

Dear God, help me to feel your stirring today. Show me where you want me to go. Tell me who you want me to touch today. Lord let me feel my heart stir for your purposes today. I love you. Amen.

Deuteronomy 4:9
*Only take heed, and guard your life diligently, lest you forget the things which your eyes have seen and lest they depart from your [mind and] heart all the days of your life. Teach them to your children and your children's children -*

We must never forget the bad from which God has pulled all of us. Every reader has a place God has rescued them out of, a bad marriage, a sickness, finances, and much more.

Don't ever forget to remind yourselves of what God has done for you. Do not ever let it depart from you. Then, make sure your children know how much God has been a part of your life and how God is there for all of us all the time!

Dear God, thank you specifically for pulling my marriage out of the throws of divorce. Lord, help me never forget your restorative powers. Lord, help to show my children how miraculous and awesome you are. I love you. Amen.

Deuteronomy 4:29
*But if from there you will seek (inquire for and require as necessity) the Lord your God, you will find Him if you [truly] seek Him with all your heart [and mind] and soul and life.*

We can't just show up on Sunday mornings and think that's all we need for the week for God. We must seek him everyday and all day. We need make him a life necessity.

We are to seek God on all levels. We need to seek him in our hearts. We must seek him in our minds. Our lives and soul must seek him too. Then, you will truly find the Lord on every level of your life.

Dear God, I seek you on all levels of my life today. I give you my heart, I ask for you to broaden my mind, and Lord let my life and soul be all that you planned it to. I love you. Amen.

<u>Deuteronomy 30:14</u>
*But the word is very near you, in your
mouth and in your mind and in your heart,
so that you can do it.*

The word is the scripture of the Bible. The
word is our daily bread. Do we like to go
a day with out food? The words of God
should be our spiritual food for everyday.

The words God inspired and breathed upon
are the only thing that will sustain you. We
must read the word and then digest it. How
that happens is you read the word, apply it
to your life, and then remember it in your
heart so that you can do it.

Dear God, help me to read your word
everyday. Lord, now I know it is vital to
my well being on earth. The word is like
the food I must eat everyday. Lord, help
me to digest your words, put it in my heart,
and then act on what I know. I love you.
Amen.

<u>1 Kings 8:61</u>
*Let your hearts therefore be blameless
and wholly true to the Lord our God,
to walk in His statutes and to keep His
commandments, as today.*

God looks only at our hearts. The only
way to keep our hearts pure and blameless
is to obey God. This does not mean we will
not mess up. This does not mean we will
not sin. But if God knows our intentions
are pure and holy, then He will not blame
us.

Starting today, try to really walk out the
words you hear and read from the Bible.
Many read and study the word but never do
the word. Make sure you are being doers of
the word so that your hearts can be called
blameless.

Dear God, help me not just to read and
hear your words BUT to do what you have
commanded. Lord, help me to walk in
obedience to your will. I love you. Amen.

Psalm 5:3

*In the morning You hear my voice, O Lord;
in the morning I prepare [a prayer, a
sacrifice] for You and watch and wait [for
You to speak to my heart].*

This just gives me God bumps like chill
bumps. The Lord hears us. This fact still
just bring tears to my eyes that the Lord of
all creation hears my little voice among the
billions.

What are you sacrificing in your life for
him today? Are you giving him extra
minutes in the day? Are you reaching out
to others? Are you listening for him to
speak in a still quiet place? Just remember,
God hears you. Wait for him to speak to
you too.

Dear God, how awesome it is that you
hear me. Lord, help me put more of you in
my everyday life. Lord, help me to be still
and to listen for you to speak. I love you.
Amen.

<u>Psalm 7:10</u>
*My defense and shield depend on God,*
*Who saves the upright in heart.*

An upright heart can be defined as: being in accord with what is right. The question we must ask today is, "Can God count on you to do what He desires?" Are our hearts in tune to do what we know is right and of God?

God says right here that He will be our defense and our shield if we have an upright heart. Today, I need God on a desperate level to defend me. Therefore, I ask God to give my heart a check and to make sure my heart is what it should be. As David said, "Cleanse my heart oh God". Do you need God as your defender? Then ask him for a heart check today.

Dear God, I too ask to cleanse my heart. Make sure Lord, my heart is in tune to what you want. Lord, help me to in accord to what is right so that you will be shield and my defender. I love you. Amen.

<u>Psalm 10:17</u>
*O Lord, You have heard the desire and the
longing of the humble and oppressed; You
will prepare and strengthen and direct their
hearts, You will cause Your ear to hear,*

Lord I know you love the humble. Lord
your heart aches for the oppressed. Many
are oppressed today by the slavery of
the world, entrapped by prestige, lies,
materialism, and self-deceit.

Lord, help the oppressed to break free from
the bondage of the world. Lord, in the
name of Jesus and the blood of Christ bind
any enemy influence from us today. Lord,
strengthen our hearts today and direct us
towards you and away from the oppression
of the world.

Dear God, I don't want to be in bondage
to the world. Lord, release me from this
and set me free. Lord, direct my ways to
you, prepare, and strengthen my heart to do
your will. I love you. Amen.

Psalm 19:14
*Let the words of my mouth and the
meditation of my heart be acceptable
in Your sight, O Lord, my [firm,
impenetrable] Rock and my Redeemer.*

I live by this scripture daily, or at least I try to. This is my barometer scripture on how I am living my daily life. This is how I interpreted this scripture and have applied to my daily life.

Let everything that I speak be of honor and glory to God. Let my heart be pure with good intentions not evil. Lord, let me stand before you with acceptance instead of denial. Lord, please be my rock that I stand upon so that I do not fall or sink into the world of sin and evil.

Dear God, help me to watch what I say today. Let everything I speak to be good. Lord, let my heart desire to do what is right. Lord, let me come to you with out shame. Lord, I need you. I need you to be my rock so that I can endure this life until I get to heaven with you. I love you. Amen.

Psalm 27:14

*Wait and hope for and expect the Lord; be brave and of good courage and let your heart be stout and enduring. Yes, wait for and hope for and expect the Lord.*

Expect the Lord. We don't hear that much. What do you expect from God on a daily basis? Or do you wait until you are in a crisis to expect something from him?

Today ask yourself, what do I expect from God? It takes courage to believe in your expectations of God. Be strong and make the list. Most importantly, don't wait another minute to define what you need from God today!

Dear God, thank you for being a God that I can expect you to deliver what I ask and need. You tell us you answer all of our prayers if they are in alignment of you. Lord, help me to have the courage and boldness to come before you today. I love you. Amen.

<u>Psalm 31:24</u>
*Be strong and let your heart take courage,
all you who wait for and hope for and
expect the Lord!*

Some days I am so weak. Strength is
so far from me. But what I have truly
learned on a deep level is this: when I
am at my weakest I turn to God, and it is
only through him I make it. Truly, in my
weakness I become strong in his strength.

Go to God today and tell him you are
weak. Tell God all that you are struggling
with. Then ask him to rescue you in his
strength. You will develop courage to come
to God at your weakest. Be patient and
know He will be your strength in time of
need.

Dear God thank you for allowing me to lay
all of my weaknesses at your feet. I don't
have to pretend to be able to handle all
of this. Thank you for being my strength
today. I love you. Amen.

Psalm 34:18
*The Lord is close to those who are of a broken heart and saves such as are crushed with sorrow for sin and are humbly and thoroughly penitent.*

Just recently, my heart was so broken; I did not think I would ever recover. I cried everyday before my eyes even opened in the morning. I was crushed, disappointed, and the feeling of helplessness devoured my soul.

Then, humbly I went to God and said, "God you must deliver me from this pain and help my heart recover, or I can no longer go on." Within days as I awoke the tears quit flowing. A new sense of hope was birthed. The pain became less and the sorrow soon faded. God proved to me that He is close to us who have broken hearts.

Dear God, thank you for healing my broken heart. I know it will not be the last time, but now I know you will comfort me. Thank you. I love you. Amen.

<u>Psalm 37:4</u>
*Delight yourself also in the Lord, and*
*He will give you the desires and secret*
*petitions of your heart.*

We don't use delight much any more.
The definition is a high degree of pleasure
or enjoyment; joy. The question we must
ask is "Do we take pleasure and joy in the
Lord?" This is a principle of God's ways
so that He can give us the desires of our
hearts.

The best way to take pleasure in God, no
matter what your circumstances are, is to
come to God with gratefulness. I just list
all of my blessings and name them one by
one. This is a sure fire way to get God's
attention, especially in times of troubles.

Dear God, I want to delight in you. Help
me to tell you more often how thankful I
am. Help me to take pleasure in who you
are so that you can give me the desires of
my heart, even the secret wishes I hide in
my heart. I love you. Amen

Psalm 44:21
*Would not God discover this? For He knows the secrets of the heart.*

This comforts me so much. Sometimes I don't even know the secrets of my own heart, but God does. God knows everything about us and everything that is in us even when we don't know how our own heart feels.

Ask God today to reveal to you the secret needs of your heart. Thank him for being such a God that He knows your heart by name and the needs you have. God knows you so intimately that He can reveal secrets you don't even know about yourself.

Dear God, how humble I come to you today. You even know the secrets that I do not know. Amazing God, you never cease to astound me in how you love each one of us so intimately. I thank you for being this kind of loving intimate God. I love you. Amen.

<u>Psalm 51:10</u>
*Create in me a clean heart, O God, and renew a right, persevering, and steadfast spirit within me.*

This is something we need to do everyday of our lives. We need to ask God to create in us a clean heart. Just like we have to clean our clothes or dishes from use, we need to clean our hearts from what the world does to it too.

Ask God to show you where we might need some stain remover. Is there an uncovered sin? Is there a sin that you can't receive complete forgiveness of? Is there a person you have not offered forgiveness to? Ask God to clean your heart so that you will have his steadfast spirit everyday too!

Dear God, create in me a clean heart today. Lord, help me with sins I have done, shame that I carry, and the unforgiving spirit I show to those who have hurt me. Lord, wash me anew in the blood of Christ so that I can have right standing with you today. I love you. Amen.

<u>Psalm 66:18</u>
*If I regard iniquity in my heart, the Lord will not hear me;*

Iniquity is evildoing and wickedness. If we have these characteristics in our hearts then God can't hear us. The good news is that God does hear our prayers.

Ask God today to help you to keep from evil. Ask the Lord to help you not to react in wicked ways. The Lord will always deliver us from evil if we ask him. He always has a plan to get us out of trouble. But we must come to him with a humble heart and ask him to deliver us from evil and wickedness in the name of Jesus and the blood of Christ.

Dear God, please keep me safe from harm. Please keep me out the traps Satan sets for me. Lord, deliver me from evil and wickedness. I love you. Amen.

<u>Psalm 73:26</u>
*My flesh and my heart may fail, but God is the Rock and firm Strength of my heart and my Portion forever.*

Everything in this life might fail us: our husbands, families, children, bosses, and even our physical bodies, but God will never fail us! God is the one thing you will always be able to count on. God loves us even when we don't deserve it or when we are at a most unlovable place.

The Lord is our portion forever. Call upon him today and thank him for being your Rock. Thank God for being firm and strong. Thank God for never leaving or forsaking us as He promised.

Dear God, I need you. I need you as my Rock. I need your strength. Lord, though my heart and body my fail you, you never give up on me. That oh Lord, keeps me humbly bowing at your feet in praise. YOU NEVER GIVE UP ON US! I love you. Amen.

<u>Psalm 81:12</u>
*So I gave them up to their own hearts' lust and let them go after their own stubborn will, that they might follow their own counsels.*

Often I say, that God can not be where sin is living. God will leave us right in our sin. It takes me to the rich Prodigal son parable Jesus told about the son who lived in filth but then came to his senses. God will do the same. God will leave us in our sin if we remain stubborn against him.

The prodigal son was said to "come to his senses." Do you need to come to your senses today? God is waiting on you. He can't be there in the sin but He is waiting on you to come to him and ask for his counsel.

Dear God, I come to you today as a Prodigal. Please, oh Lord, let me come to my senses and start living in accordance to your will. Lord, let me not be stubborn but to humbly ask for forgiveness and follow you. I love you. Amen.

<u>Proverbs 4:23</u>
*Keep and guard your heart with all vigilance and above all that you guard, for out of it flow the springs of life.*

Your heart is the spring of life. That is where all of your life for God begins and ends, in the heart of a man. We must guard our hearts in all ways. We must keep a watch on what we allow to bring us pleasure and pain.

Do you allow evil and evil desires in your hearts such as lust and greed? Do you allow people to hurt you and you keep the offense forever? Your heart is the lifeline of your life. Make sure you are guarding it with all of your life, with your all for God.

Dear God, help me to filter what goes in and affects my heart. I know it is the life spring in which I love for you. Help me to be vigilant in keeping guard on it forever. I love you. Amen.

<u>Proverbs 12:25</u>
*Anxiety in a man's heart weighs it down,*
*but an encouraging word makes it glad.*

Anxiety can be defined as distress or uneasiness of mind caused by fear of danger or misfortune. Who has not at some time in our lives been anxious?

Just as this scripture says, it weighs a man's heart down. Is your heart heavy today? Do you have fear or feel uneasy about some areas in your life? God asks us to come to him and be anxious about nothing. I like to say, worry about NO thing and bring it all to God. Will you do this today, bring all your worries and cares to God today and leave them at his feet?

Dear God, I don't want an anxious heavy heart any longer. Lord, today I give you my list of worries and fears. Lord, I lay them all at your feet so that I may find rest in you. Lord, please make my heart light again as I see you move in your mighty way solving all of my fears and worries. I love you. Amen.

<u>Proverbs 13:12</u>
*Hope deferred makes the heart sick, but when the desire is fulfilled, it is a tree of life.*

What this means is that a life without hope will make you sick. If you do not have hope of life getting better then you will be sick. Have any of you lost hope today?

What would it take to for you to see that God can make an impossible situation completely possible? What would you need to see that things will turn out OK? That is what Hope is for you today - seeing that God can do the impossible and things can get better.

Lord, today I need to know that you can make my life change in an instant. You make the impossible happen. Lord, allow hope to overflow my heart today so that I can have a fulfilled heart. I love you. Amen.

<u>Proverbs 16:5</u>
*Everyone proud and arrogant in heart
is disgusting, hateful, and exceedingly
offensive to the Lord; be assured [I pledge
it] they will not go unpunished.*

Who in the world likes to be around
people of arrogance? Who likes to feel less
than or looked down upon? No one likes to
feel insubordinate.

On the other side, who do people think
they are to make others feel this way?
What gives them the right to even have an
opinion of others? No one has the right to
put judgments on any of us.

God hates a proud heart. He can not stand
arrogance. Scriptures say that Pride cometh
before a fall. The Lord will punish all of
those who make others feel judged.

Lord, today please do not let me come
across arrogant. Help me to reach out to
all people. Lord, don't let me judge others
even when I feel I have the right. Lord, let
me never be proud. I love you. Amen.

Proverbs 17:22

*A happy heart is good medicine and a cheerful mind works healing, but a broken spirit dries up the bones.*

When was the last time you had a good laugh? When was the last tear you shed from laughing so hard? God tells us right hear that laughter is the best medicine.

The enemy steals our laughter by keeping us down. The next time you are in a dark place or surrounded by trials, try your hardest to find something to laugh at. Sometimes one day can get so bad. I know it is the enemy, so I turn my laughter on to the devil. Often I ask the enemy as I laugh at him, "Is this the best you can come up with?"

Dear God, as I sit here with calamity and problems all around, please help me to lighten up. Help me to find some good things to smile about, so the enemy will give up. Lord, I need some good medicine of laughter today, and I know you will give it to me. I love you. Amen.

<u>Proverbs 23:7</u>
*For as he thinks in his heart, so is he.*

Your heart tells everything about you. You can lie and deceive yourself for a period of time, but in the end your heart will be what you are.

What is your heart thinking today? Do you long for healing? Are you full of joy that overflows? Do you have peace that passes all understanding?

If you want to know how true this scripture is, ask a truthful friend to describe how you are most of the time. Would they say you are grumpy, sad, happy, or calm? That will indicate and tell you what your heart is!

Dear God, don't let me lie to myself about who I am. Lord, let my heart be pure and good so that I may be what my heart indicates. I love you. Amen.

<u>Luke 5:22</u>
*But Jesus, knowing their thoughts and questionings, answered them, Why do you question in your hearts?*

This scripture shows that Jesus knows what is inside of us. It says He knew their thoughts. How many of us fool ourselves into thinking that no one knows what are thoughts and motives are?

Jesus and God are the same way; they know exactly what you intentions are. Don't think just because you go to church you are a Christian. God knows why we do things or why we don't do things. So, today don't kid yourself in your intentions.

Dear God, help me to have good intentions. Lord, touch my heart in such a way all I want to do is good. Lord, you know my innermost thoughts. I love you. Amen.

<u>Luke 10:27</u>
*And he replied, You must love the Lord your God with all your heart and with all your soul and with all your strength and with all your mind; and your neighbor as yourself.*

You can't just love God when it feels good. Sometimes when we feel the worst, that is when we need to reach out to him the most. We must give God our all - all the time.

We must love him with our hearts and in our thoughts. We must love him with all of our strength, and our intentions must be pure. Then most importantly, we must love our neighbors as we love ourselves. Do you love yourself? We can't love others until we love ourselves.

Dear God, help me to love myself. Lord, help me to forgive myself and accept who I am. Lord, I am your child. Thank you for loving me. Lord, help me to love you with my entire life. Lord, help me to love others as I love myself and you. I love you. Amen.

Luke 12:34
*For where your treasure is, there will your heart be also.*

I love this scripture today. You can tell where people's trust and their interest in the world is by what they do. You can tell a person by the way they spend their time.

You can also tell what people treasure the most by how they spend their money. Do they spend on all the material things, themselves? Or do they try and find places to give their money to help others?

Where would people say you spend your time and money? Would it be for the Kingdom's benefit or yours? Where is your treasure? It is where you have your heart focused.

Dear God, let me be a person who treasures what you treasure. Help me to give to the needy and give my time and money to those you lead me to. Lord, help me not to be selfish and store treasures down here on earth. I love you. Amen.

<u>Luke 15:10</u>

*Even so, I tell you, there is joy among*
*and in the presence of the angels of God*
*over one [especially] wicked person*
*who repents (changes his mind for the*
*better, heartily amending his ways, with*
*abhorrence of his past sins).*

This scripture keeps me motivated to
my ministry more than any other. In
the beginning of ministry I brought the
world's standard of success by counting in
numbers. How many attended what event
and where.

God is more interested in our reaching
one person who repents and changes his
life than the many who act as though they
don't need forgiveness at all. God and the
angels rejoice when the one changes.

Dear God, help me to reach out to the one
person who needs you. Help me to look
everyday for the one person in pain. Lord, I
am grateful that you rejoice over one more
than all the others who don't need you.
Thank you for not being a God of numbers.
I love you. Amen.

John 14:1
*DO NOT let your hearts be troubled
(distressed, agitated). You believe in and
adhere to and trust in and rely on God;
believe in and adhere to and trust in and
rely also on me.*

Sometimes we all get agitated. Sometimes
our hearts get in distress, and we don't
know what to do. God calls us to not be
troubled not be distressed. But when we
are, this is when God is at his best.

God loves to rescue his own. God is a God
of plans. He is one who can be trusted
with everything. We must believe that
God can fix and do anything, and then He
will show up. Faith in God activates his
actions!

Dear God, thank you for your rescue.
Thank you for fixing broken hearts. Lord,
I call upon you in times of distress, and
I trust and believe that you will pull me
through victoriously every time. I love
you. Amen.

John 15:7
*If you live in Me [abide vitally united to Me] and My words remain in you and continue to live in your hearts, ask whatever you will, and it shall be done for you.*

We must stay with God and remain in him always. Our hearts must always be rechecked and concentrated on God. We must stay united with God good times and bad. Then He will answer your prayers.

Today ask God to help you abide in him closer. Ask God to keep the world out of your heart. Ask God to come into your heart daily and establish your day for you. Then God will answer whatever you need because He knows that it will be in alignment of him.

Dear God, search my heart and come closer to me. Lord, I want to be in unity with you. Thank you Lord, that you answer all of my prayers according to your will. I love you. Amen.

<u>Psalm 36:7</u>
*How precious is Your steadfast love, O God! The children of men take refuge and put their trust under the shadow of Your wings.*

That is one fact that reassures me. We serve an awesome God! He is steadfast in his love for us! His love is unwavering and faithful to us. No matter how many times we fail God He is right there to pick us up and love on us.

Today take refuge in this one fact. Come to God and soak in his presence of forgiveness, grace, mercy, and unfailing love. Trust upon him all your needs and hide in the shadow of God Almighty's wings.

Thank you, Lord, for loving me even when I sin and when I sin again. Thank you, Lord, for never giving up on me. Lord, I take refuge in you today. I feel your touch as I hide in the shadow of your wings and protection. I love you. Amen.

Psalm 59:10
*My God in His mercy and steadfast
love will meet me; God will let me look
[triumphantly] on my enemies (those who
lie in wait for me).*


God knows when we choose to follow him
it is not easy. On top of that He also knows
we will have enemies who will try and trip
us up. God will never let your enemies
defeat you.

God will make you triumphant over your
enemies. God will defend you and be
your shield. God knows that everything
goes against those that truly follow his
commandments. God will never let us lose
to our enemies. We will always savor a
sweet victory in Christ.

Dear Father, thank you for knowing how
tough it can be down here. Lord, thank you
for protecting me from those who mean
to cause me harm. Lord, thank you for the
victory of Jesus Christ and his death on the
cross, defeating the world and death for all
of us. I love you. Amen.

<u>Isaiah 30:18</u>
*And therefore the Lord [earnestly] waits
[expecting, looking, and longing] to be
gracious to you; and therefore He lifts
Himself up, that He may have mercy on you
and show loving-kindness to you. For the
Lord is a God of justice. Blessed (happy,
fortunate, to be envied) are all those who
[earnestly] wait for Him, who expect and
look and long for Him [for His victory, His
favor, His love, His peace, His joy, and His
matchless, unbroken companionship]!*

Today just look for God's companionship.
Thank him for the intimate friendship
Accept his mercy and love and wait for
him in all you do.

God will show favor, love, and peace onto
us.

Dear God, I wait for you. I expect your
kindness, love and mercy. I know I will be
happy and blessed because of your love
and friendship that we have. I love you.
Amen.

<u>Zephaniah 3:17</u>
*The Lord your God is in the midst of you,
a Mighty One, a Savior [Who saves]! He
will rejoice over you with joy; He will rest
[in silent satisfaction] and in His love He
will be silent and make no mention [of past
sins, or even recall them]; He will exult
over you with singing.*

God is a God who saves! The Bible tells
us that when his people struggled so hard
to do as He commanded, He allowed his
only Son, Jesus to be born to bridge the
gap. Praise God for that. Jesus and the
blood He shed for us brought us forever in
communion with God.

What is most amazing is that when we
confess our sins, God will make no
mention of them again. God will forget
your sins and never recall them.

Dear God, thank you for Jesus so that
we can be in a real relationship with you.
Thank you so much for forgiving me and
not remembering my sins ever again. I love
you. Amen.

Matthew 6:24

*No one can serve two masters; for either he will hate the one and love the other, or he will stand by and be devoted to the one and despise and be against the other. You cannot serve God and mammon (deceitful riches, money, possessions, or whatever is trusted in).*

This is truer today than ever. We can't live in the world and say we follow Christ. We can't submit to the world's standards then call ourselves spiritual. This will not work.

You can not serve the world, live like the world, and serve God. You can't collect all the worldly possessions and attitudes and be obedient to God.

Are you serving God or man? Who do you care about the most?

Dear God, I want to serve only you. I want to be devoted to you alone. Keep my heart from being influenced by the world. I love you. Amen.

John 3:16

*For God so greatly loved and dearly prized the world that He [even] gave up His only begotten (unique) Son, so that whoever believes in (trusts in, clings to, relies on) Him shall not perish (come to destruction, be lost) but have eternal (everlasting) life.*

How many of you reading this today have children? If you do, can you imagine knowing from the time of their conception that He would have to be hung on a cross cruelly left to die? Can you imagine the pain God experienced watching his Son cry out in agony and desperation and not be able to do anything so that the world could be saved?

God gave us, you and me, his Son for us to be in relationship with him. Choose Jesus so that you will not perish but have eternal life with God.

Dear Father, thank you for allowing Jesus to suffer on the cross for my sin. I am so sorry for my sins. Lord, forgive me and love me. I love you. Amen.

<u>Romans 5:5</u>
*Such hope never disappoints or deludes or shames us, for God's love has been poured out in our hearts through the Holy Spirit Who has been given to us.*

Do you know what really lives inside of you? Once we believe in Jesus and He takes residence in our hearts, the Holy Spirit resides inside of you too. The power is waiting for you to call upon it.

God's love, knowledge, and will are revealed to us through the Spirit. Our hearts open the door to the Spirit pouring out of us.

Dear God, let me call upon the power inside of me. Lord, I acknowledge that I am just flesh that houses a part of your spirit within my heart. Lord, help me to know who you are through the power I have to do all things through Christ that strengthens me.
I love you Amen.

Romans 5:8

*But God shows and clearly proves His [own] love for us by the fact that while we were still sinners, Christ (the Messiah, the Anointed One) died for us.*

God loves us so much He allowed his Son to die on a cross for us. God didn't wait on us to make things right. God came to rescue us when we were still sinning in darkness.

Don't wait until you get all cleaned up or your life straight before you come to God. God loves you so much his Son died for you. Come to him as you are; He already knows all that you are anyway. You can't hide anything from God.

Dear God, I come to you today as a sinner. Please forgive me for all of my sins. Lord, thank you that Jesus died on the cross for me. Lord, I come to you broken, and I know you will make me whole. I love you. Amen.

<u>Romans 8:39</u>
*Nor height nor depth, nor anything else in all creation will be able to separate us from the love of God which is in Christ Jesus our Lord.*

This is a scripture that God has put a mandate on my life to share each time I speak. NOTHING, Nothing, will ever separate you from the love of God.

The enemy loves to make us think that God does not love us because we have sinned. But we all have fallen short and sinned when it comes to God. That is a lie from the enemy because he wants us to hide in shame from God. The enemy wants us to feel like God can't love us in our sin. As I always say, God loves the sinner not the sin.

Lord, I come to you and thank you for not leaving me when I fail you. I am so sorry that the enemy has lied to me so long making me feel you are not near. Thank you for not giving up on me. I love you. Amen.

<u>2 Thessalonians 3:5</u>
*May the Lord direct your hearts into*
*[realizing and showing] the love of God*
*and into the steadfastness and patience of*
*Christ and in waiting for His return.*

I don't know about you but sometimes I plead with God to just come on and get us! I get so impatient when I am down and out or under trials. I am so thankful God is steadfast and patient with us.

Can you imagine if God just ran out of patience with us? Then, we truly would have no hope in his return for us. Today, I ask for patience in waiting for his return and thank him for the hope in the fact He is coming to take us out of here.

Dear God, please forgive me when I get restless and weary. Forgive me when I get anxious to get out of here. Lord, thank you that you never lose patience with us. Thank you that you are coming to get us on judgment day. I love you. Amen.

<u>2 Timothy 1:7</u>
*For God did not give us a spirit of timidity
(of cowardice, of craven and cringing
and fawning fear), but [He has given us a
spirit] of power and of love and of calm
and well-balanced mind and discipline and
self-control.*

Why is it that the enemy loves for us to be
timid and fearful? Why is it when things are
at the roughest, the enemy tells us the worst
is going to happen?

God is not a God who gives us a spirit of
fear or timidity. We are to go to him every
time the enemy starts that taunting and ask
God to make him flee. I tell people to think
of the worst that could happen in a situation
where you are scared. Then they see that
the worst is not so bad! Most of the tears of
worry I have cried never even happened

Dear God, today help me to get rid of fear.
Help me to see you are not a God of fear.
Lord, help me find safety and confidence in
you today. Tell the enemy to flee from me
today. I love you. Amen.

<u>James 1:12</u>
*Blessed (happy, to be envied) is the man
who is patient under trial and stands up
under temptation, for when he has stood
the test and been approved, he will receive
[the victor's] crown of life which God has
promised to those who love Him.*

I read this and find it hard to believe many
of my friends or family would ever envy the
trials of fire I have overcome lately! But, it
is a great feeling to know that I did stand up
to the temptations and tests.

I have found that God works this way in
my life. God allows trials and tests, and He
knows that what is burnt off or strengthened
would be the first weakness that might
cause you to stumble. The next time you are
under a trial ask God, "What do I need to
learn from this?" God will show you what
to do.

Dear God, I know that trials are what make
me who I need to be. Lord, each test brings
more of you out in me. Lord, I give you all
the glory of my victories over Satan. I love
you. Amen.

<u>1 John 3:1</u>
*See what [an incredible] quality of love the
Father has given (shown, bestowed on) us,
that we should [be permitted to] be named
and called and counted the children of God!
And so we are! The reason that the world
does not know (recognize, acknowledge)
us is that it does not know (recognize,
acknowledge) Him.*

I still shout to know that I am truly God's
daughter. God created me before I was even
conceived in my mother's womb. God had
a specific job for me when He formed me.
To be counted as God's own child makes me
jump for joy.

Allow God to give you a touch of joy in
knowing not only who you are but WHOSE
you are! You are God's own. He formed you
and created you for purpose. Feel him with a
smile on your face today to know you are his.

Dear God, I thank you for making me yours
and with a specific purpose no one else can
do. Lord, I feel you in the happiness in my
heart as I declare I am yours.

<u>1 John 4:10</u>
*In this is love: not that we loved God, but*
*that He loved us and sent His Son to be the*
*propitiation (the atoning sacrifice) for our*
*sins.*

God loved us first! God knew we would
bring him heart ache, that we would fall
short of his commandments. God knew we
would wonder and wander from him, but He
still stayed on his plan of redemption.

God loved us so much that He allowed
Jesus, a perfect, sinless man, his only Son, to
die on a cross for us! There is no such love
as this. It is a love that is incomprehensible.
Thankfully it is available to all who will
give their life over to him and confess that
Jesus is the Son of the living God.

Dear God, I can't even comprehend the
love you have for me. You watched in
overwhelming grief as your only Son lay
dying on a blood soaked cross. But you
knew the only way to bring man into heaven
was through your Son. I thank you Father,
for your supernatural love. I love you.

*Day 162*

<u>Psalm 94:19</u>
*In the multitude of my [anxious] thoughts within me, Your comforts cheer and delight my soul!*

Lord, you are the only place to find comfort. Not enough alcohol, drugs, smoking, or shallow relationships can comfort as you do. I may search in all of these wrong places. I may find a temporary fix, but you, God, are the only permanent place to find comfort for my soul.

Lord today, I ask you to replace all of the worldly choices I have used to try and ease the pain and to comfort. Lord, I know you are the only place to find true peace and comfort. Lord, thank you for being there and for always being willing to be my comfort in a way that nothing else compares. Thank you for healing my pains and broken hearts. I love you. Amen.

<u>Psalm 127:2</u>
*It is vain for you to rise up early, to take
rest late, to eat the bread of [anxious] toil
- for He gives [blessings] to His beloved in
sleep.*

Here the Lord lets us know that we need
not to work in vain. The world has us under
such an influence that we must work all the
time to get ahead or to get promoted. God
says just the opposite. God calls us to rest
and toil not in vain.

Ask yourself today, "Do I work so hard
now so that I can get ahead or to chase
away the fear of uncertainty?" Have you
come under the wrong influence that you
must work at a crazy pace and for long
hours to get what you think you deserve?
God says He gives blessings to us, his
beloved sheep.

Dear God, please help me to slow down.
Lord, break the curse of the thought that I
must work myself long hours. I need you
to help me trust in you, that you will give
more than enough for all of my needs. I
love you. Amen.

## Matthew 6:25-26

*25Therefore I tell you, stop being [d] perpetually uneasy (anxious and worried) about your life, what you shall eat or what you shall drink; or about your body, what you shall put on. Is not life greater [in quality] than food, and the body [far above and more excellent] than clothing? 26Look at the birds of the air; they neither sow nor reap nor gather into barns, and yet your heavenly Father keeps feeding them. Are you not worth much more than they?*

Lord, thank you for letting me see I worry so much about too much. I know I am more valuable to you than a bird. Lord, help me to concentrate on my inner man and to be more like you. Lord, I know you will supply all of my needs, and I will never lack for anything because I am a child of the King.

Dear God, thank you for providing all that I need. Lord, help me not to worry about clothes and food. I know you will give me more than I need. I love you. Amen.

Matthew 6:34

*So do not worry or be anxious about tomorrow, for tomorrow will have worries and anxieties of its own. Sufficient for each day is its own trouble.*

Isn't this the truth? My today has enough worry in its own right. I have learned to truly ask God to just get me through this day.

Again so much of what we have established is earthly teachings about saving for tomorrow, planning for retirement years, and always looking ahead. God does not do this. God says look at today, and He will give you what you need for this day, and tomorrow will take care of itself.

Dear God, help my wrong thinking today. Help me to just look at today and what all today brings. Lord, help me to trust that you have tomorrow covered. Help me to see you break me away from always planning the future and worrying. I love you. Amen.

<u>Matthew 26:38</u>
*Then He said to them, My soul is very sad and deeply grieved, so that I am almost dying of sorrow. Stay here and keep awake and keep watch with Me.*

This was Jesus saying these words. His soul was sad. Jesus was deeply grieved. He says He felt as though He may die from the sorrow. Have you ever been this way? I have been so broken; I thought I might never recover.

It is so comforting to know when I am so low and so sad that Jesus knows exactly how I feel. My sweet Jesus felt it too. So today if you feel betrayed, disappointed, or broken hearted, take comfort that Jesus has been there too. Jesus hurt so bad that He felt like He might die from sorrow.

Dear God, thank you that you allowed Jesus to live like a man but without sin. Jesus knows all the pains and hurts this life gives, and He can heal us from them too. Thank you for knowing exactly where my pain hurts. I love you. Amen.

Psalm 34:18

*The Lord is close to those who are of a broken heart and saves such as are crushed with sorrow for sin and are humbly and thoroughly penitent.*

I have had to experience this on such a deep personal level. In one week my child, my ministry, coworkers, and others all disappointed and betrayed me. My heart was so broken I thought I would never recover. I was so crushed that I wasn't sure I could pull myself literally back together.

When I saw this scripture, it gave me such hope. I just knew that God was with me. I knew He was close, and I could see in my spirit that He was crying right there beside me. As a Mom, I have cried many tears next to my child as life handed them a blow and hurt them. We are God's child, and He does the same too.

Dear God, thank you that you cry right with me. You know my pain and heal me from it. I love you. Amen.

Lamentations 3:32
*But though He causes grief, yet will He be moved to compassion according to the multitude of His loving-kindness and tender mercy.*

Compassion can be defined as a strong desire to alleviate the suffering. This is a lost trait in the world today. How many of us hear a person describe another very often as compassionate?

That's my challenge for us today - to feel the presence of God by working on ourselves to be more compassionate. Jesus was so compassionate it led him to heal so many because He could not stand by and not do anything to help. Let's all work on this trait as a Christ follower - to be more compassionate towards our fellow man.

Dear God, thank you for your compassion. Thank you for always trying to alleviate our suffering. We know you will work all things out for your good and glory. I love you. Amen.

<u>2 Corinthians 7:10</u>
*For godly grief and the pain God is permitted to direct, produce a repentance that leads and contributes to salvation and deliverance from evil, and it never brings regret; but worldly grief (the hopeless sorrow that is characteristic of the pagan world) is deadly [breeding and ending in death].*

I love to boast on God and say that God's pain is never wasted. God's pain always brings about change. There is purpose in God's pain. As soon as you acknowledge that God will allow pain only if He knows you will bear it and come out victorious, then you can ask what to learn from the painful experience. Today if you are in pain, know that God has a reason for it. Ask him to show you what to learn from it.

Dear God, thank you for helping me learn a new way. Thank you for teaching me through the pain life brings. Show me your ways oh Lord, and I know where to go. Thank you for always turning my pain to gain. I love you Amen.

<u>Revelation 21:4</u>
*God will wipe away every tear from their eyes; and death shall be no more, neither shall there be anguish (sorrow and mourning) nor grief nor pain any more, for the old conditions and the former order of things have passed away.*

There will be a day, no matter what the world tells you, when God is coming back. He will wipe away all pain and tears. There will be no more death, no more sorrow, no more anguish, and no more injustice. God says He will make everything new again.

Are you ready for this day? Is Jesus in your heart as your Lord and Savior? Ask him today to be your Savior and to bring you in a deeper relationship today.

Dear God, thank you for the hope of heaven. Thank you that one day I truly will live without pain, death, sorrow, injustice, and that all will be new. I live for the day you return. I love you. Amen.

<u>Psalm 147:3</u>
*He heals the brokenhearted and binds up their wounds [curing their pains and their sorrows].*

God truly does heal. Many doubt this fact but He does heal. The scriptures say that God is the same yesterday, today, and tomorrow a God who never changes. Do you believe this? You must!

By the measure we believe is the measure of result you will get. What do you need from God today? Ask for it and then believe with everything you are that He will deliver it to you. God truly heals and binds the broken hearted wounds.

Dear God, help me to believe with all that I am that you do still heal. Lord, I ask you to heal me (tell him where), and Lord, I believe you will. Thank you, Lord, for binding my wounds and curing all of my pains and sorrows. I love you. Amen.

<u>Luke 22:62</u>
*And He went out and wept bitterly [that is, with painfully moving grief].*

Again today, we see Jesus weep bitterly. What does this mean? Jesus had such pain it was hard to bear. Do we really acknowledge that often enough? Do we realize Jesus was human just like us BUT was perfect and without sin. Because He was human, He still felt all of the five senses we do.

Today try and feel God's presence by acknowledging Jesus cried, laughed, wept, and felt all of the things on earth as we do. When we need a shoulder to cry on, someone to laugh with, or someone to celebrate with, Jesus is right there waiting to be with you.

Dear God, thank you for letting me see that Jesus felt all the things I do, but He did not make any mistakes. Thank you for allowing me to see today that I can turn to Jesus with anything and He will know exactly what I am feeling. I love you. Amen.

<u>Hebrews 4:10</u>
*For He who has once entered [God's] rest
also has ceased from [the weariness and
pain] of human labors, just as God rested
from those labors peculiarly His own.*

This is so hard to do, to rest in God. Just
rest in waiting for Him, acknowledging He
knows best. To take rest in God with our
injustice or pain is so hard.

How do we rest in God? We must first
acknowledge He is in complete control. We
must know that He has a plan and a destiny
for us. We must use our Holy Spirit to trust
God and not allow our human eyes to keep
seeing just the storm. God is the calm in the
storm. Give him control and allow the Holy
Spirit to show you that God's ways are
always best, so you will find rest in God.

Lord, thank you for being our rest. Help
me to relinquish control of my life. Lord, I
surrender to you today and allow my Spirit
to look beyond what my human eyes see.
Lord, I will find rest in you today. I love
you. Amen.

Revelation 21:4
*God will wipe away every tear from
their eyes; and death shall be no more,
neither shall there be anguish (sorrow and
mourning) nor grief nor pain any more, for
the old conditions and the former order of
things have passed away.*

Again, such HOPE that old things will
pass and new things are here to stay. All of
us love new things: new cars, new houses,
new clothes, new shoes, and new toys. In
heaven, all things are new. All of the old
will be washed away.

Today when you get weary and tired and
the same OLD problems are still around,
hold on to this fact - one day all will be
new to us! I have such hope when I realize
one day that I will start all new.

Dear God, thank you that all the old will
pass away when you come for your final
day of judgment. Thank you for letting me
feel this hope today. I am ready to wipe
away all of the old and spend eternity in
the new with you. I love you. Amen.

<u>Exodus 14:14</u>
*The Lord will fight for you, and you shall hold your peace and remain at rest.*

What an encouraging word today that God fights for us. It doesn't say when you do something or if you are in perfect alignment with God, He will fight for you. No it says God will fight for you and there are no conditions.

The Lord is our shield. The Lord is our defender. There is no other defender that we need but God. What is it you need the Lord to fight for you today? Are you fighting to quit an addiction, a losing relationship, a wayward teen? God says to you today, He is fighting for you!

Dear God, thank you for fighting for me. In that Lord today I will feel you because I will rest in you. I will find peace in the fact you are fighting for me, so now I can rest. I love you. Amen.

<u>Exodus 24:16</u>
*The glory of the Lord rested on Mount Sinai, and the cloud covered it for six days. On the seventh day [God] called to Moses out of the midst of the cloud.*

God can call you from anywhere. He can call you from the skies or from a sermon or from a friend. The fact is that God longs to speak to all of us. God will rest on you and tell you what you need to know.

Are you still enough to hear God? Do you set aside a time of day to just be before him in silence or in prayer? If you will, God will come and speak to you and you will be so blessed for making time for God.

Dear God, help me to be still. Lord, I know you have so much to tell me. Help me to listen and set a time each day to just be with you. I love you. Amen.

<u>Exodus 33:14</u>
*And the Lord said, My Presence shall go with you, and I will give you rest.*

Thank you, Lord, that wherever I go, you are with me. Sometimes Lord, I feel so alone and scared, but now I will remember you are with me. Your presence will be in the way I feel or what my ears might hear.

Lord, help me to be aware all the time of your presence. Lord, help me to see, hear, taste, smell, and touch you in way that will affirm that you are near. Thank you that you never leave your children alone.

Dear God, forgive me that I forget you are with me all the time. Lord, give me a better sense of your presence. Lord, I will feel you today as I rest in the knowledge that you are with me at all times. Lord, thank you for calling me your own. I love you. Amen.

Numbers 11:25

*And the Lord came down in the cloud and spoke to him, and took of the Spirit that was upon him and put It upon the seventy elders; and when the Spirit rested upon them, they prophesied [sounding forth the praises of God and declaring His will]. Then they did so no more.*

Do you allow God to speak through you? Do you sometimes feel like you should say something but choose not to? Do you feel like you know the answer for a friend, but you don't share the solution for fear they may not understand?

God will use you to speak in people's lives. When you are in the word and alignment with God, He will use your opinions and solutions to affirm and help those around you. Be bold next time and watch God work through your speaking his will.

Dear God, help me to be bold when I know I need to speak. Lord, help me little by little to tell others around me what I hear you say to me. I love you. Amen.

<u>Job 24:23</u>
*God gives them security, and they rest on it; and His eyes are upon their ways.*

Thank you, Lord, today now that I know your eyes are on me. You see the place I am in right now. Thank you for this, so I know I don't have to hide anything from you. Lord, I know you don't want any of us to suffer.

Lord, today let me find security in just knowing you are watching me. Lord, to know you are seeing my life as it is. Lord, today I rest that you know exactly and precisely where I am today.

Dear God, I am so glad you see me just as I am. I don't have to hide or proclaim anything about my life to you. Lord, thank you for giving me security and rest. I love you. Amen.

Psalm 19:7
*The law of the Lord is perfect, restoring the [whole] person; the testimony of the Lord is sure, making wise the simple.*

The Lord is perfect. He is best when we are at our worst. The Lord loves incredible odds not in your favor. Just at the last point, right before a complete failure, God moves in. God comes in, and the whole situation changes in an instant!

That gives us a testimony, a story to tell others how God works in miraculous ways! That is why I give God my all each and every day because my testimony is that God restored and replaced so much in my life against all odds. God is no respecter of persons. That means He will do it for you too!

Dear God, you know my situation looks impossible but Lord you are the God of miracles. Lord, thank you that I know you can do anything - all things are possible with you. I need it today. I love you. Amen.

<u>Psalm 23:3</u>
*He refreshes and restores my life (my self);*
*He leads me in the paths of righteousness*
*[uprightness and right standing with Him*
*- not for my earning it, but] for His name's*
*sake.*

Lord, you do refresh my soul. Suddenly when I am at my end, you step in and give me a great idea to solve my issue. Lord, you restore my hope daily as I come to you humbly asking you to forgive me, and I know you do.

Lord, you make me righteous because it's through Jesus' blood I stand before you, right standing with God. Thank you for leading me and guiding me even when I don't acknowledge it.

Dear God, today I feel you because I will be restored. You will give me a new plan, a new word, or a new song in my mouth. Thank you for the blood of the Christ where I can be called righteous before you. I love you. Amen.

<u>Psalm 37:7</u>
*Be still and rest in the Lord; wait for Him
and patiently lean yourself upon Him; fret
not yourself because of him who prospers
in his way*

Lord, help me to rest in you. Lord, help
me to be patient. I know that it's when
I am patient is when you are doing your
most work for me. In the time of patience,
I develop character, I learn to wait, and I
know it's not me working. In patience I
know God when the outcome is realized.
That is all you and not something of my
own work.

Lord, I know that all things that are good
are from you. You are a God who loves to
prosper his own. You love to give gifts to
those who are patient.

Dear God, as I wait upon you today I am
learning patience and that it is all you who
will make it happen. Lord, I know your
plans are good for me, and you love to give
me gifts because I am your child. I love
you. Amen.

Psalm 140:12
*I know and rest in confidence upon it that*
*the Lord will maintain the cause of the*
*afflicted, and will secure justice for the*
*poor and needy [of His believing children].*

Do you believe in God? Do you really
believe God can heal and help the
afflicted? We must believe. It is our faith
that activated God to do his miraculous
power. The opposite of faith is fear and we
can't live in fear. We must act on faith.

My biggest question to many is, "What
have you got to lose?" "Why not err on the
side of the Lord and his miraculous powers
than err on the side of man and fear?

Dear God, I want to error on your side.
I want to believe you can heal, restore,
and replenish anything. Lord, help me to
squelch my fear. Lord, I know you care for
the afflicted and can make us whole. I love
you. Amen.

<u>Matthew 11:28</u>
*Come to Me, all you who labor and are heavy-laden and overburdened, and I will cause you to rest. [I will ease and relieve and refresh your souls.]*

God desires for us to put all of our cares and burdens on him. He wants us to put our anxiousness on him too. He knows how hard it is to not let the cares of our natural lives affect us.

God is asking you today, will you put your cares, stress and worry on him today? Will you lay it all at his feet today? Will you allow God to be your rest and relieve your burdened heart? God can refresh your soul and lighten your load.

Dear God, I lay it all down today. I list today all the worry and burdens, and I will leave them at your feet. Lord, I will feel you today as I acknowledge that my heart is lighter and in the process of being refreshed. I love you. Amen.

<u>1 Corinthians 2:5</u>
*So that your faith might not rest in the wisdom of men (human philosophy), but in the power of God.*

We all have been blinded by the world's philosophy. It tells us that this life is all about us. Also, whoever dies with the most toys wins. Also, that God will give you another chance after you die here on earth. It's all wrong.

The only power of life and choice is in God and his timing. God is the only place to find rest and wisdom. Don't be fooled; don't wait another minute to declare him as Lord and his Son as the Son of the Living God, because there is not a chance after you die.

Dear God, help my mind not to entertain what the world tells me. Lord, I know chasing after what the world offers only leads to eternal death. Lord, I claim you, as my Lord Savior, and I know I will dwell with you in heaven forever. I love you. Amen.

<u>Hebrews 4:3</u>

*For we who have believed (adhered to and trusted in and relied on God) do enter that rest, in accordance with His declaration that those [who did not believe] should not enter when He said, As I swore in My wrath, They shall not enter My rest; and this He said although [His] works had been completed and prepared [and waiting for all who would believe] from the foundation of the world.*

Worry is the number one enemy tactic we see today. War, uncertain economy, job losses, and more, the enemy dwells all of this upon us daily. Today we must come to God for rest because the fight is so strong.

Only God's children will find rest. The world will stay in darkness and turmoil. But God has been preparing rest for all of us since the foundation of the world.

Dear God, I want to find rest today. Help me to defend against the enemy when he slings worry on me. Thank you for preparing rest for me. I love you. Amen.

<u>Hebrews 4:11</u>
*Let us therefore be zealous and exert ourselves and strive diligently to enter that rest [of God, to know and experience it for ourselves], that no one may fall or perish by the same kind of unbelief and disobedience [into which those in the wilderness fell].*

It seems an oxymoron to seek diligently for rest doesn't it? That we need to exert and be zealous to find rest from God. Sometimes we have to fight to get to the rest. Lack of sleep, interrupted days, and broken hearts are all symptoms of needing rest.

God wants us to desire his rest, and if you seek it, you will get it. Believe that He is ready to give it you. All you have to do is fight to get to his presence and then leave it all there, so He in turn can give you a much needed rest.

Dear God, I'm in a fight with the devil to find you and find your rest. Today I leave you my fight and my worries so that you can give me rest. I love you. Amen.

<u>Revelation 14:11</u>
*And the smoke of their torment ascends forever and ever; and they have no respite (no pause, no intermission, no rest, no peace) day or night - these who pay homage to the beast and to his image and whoever receives the stamp of his name upon him.*

Whom are you serving today man or God? Are you worried about what the world thinks or what God thinks? You must answer this question today.

If you ever want eternal peace and rest, you must serve God! If you serve man and the world that is under the beast and his power, you will never find rest or peace. You will live in torment forever.

Dear God, I want to serve you. Help me to keep you the center of my life. Lord, help me to reach others who are serving the beast so that they will not have to live in torment forever. I love you. Amen.

<u>Deuteronomy 32:4</u>
*He is the Rock, His work is perfect, for all His ways are law and justice. A God of faithfulness without breach or deviation, just and right is He.*

Justice is something we all are in jeopardy of losing. Our court systems are so messed up. There is so little justice served anymore. But our God is a God of justice. He is faithful without breach or deviation.

God does not have certain rules for certain people. God treats all of us the same. Rich or poor, young or old, God gives us all the same judgments.

Dear God, thank you for being a God of justice. It is so good to know that we all will be judged and treated the same. You will not lie or change your justice system. Today Lord, I thank you for the peace from that knowledge. I love you. Amen.

<u>Job 11:20</u>
*But the eyes of the wicked shall look [for relief] in vain, and they shall not escape [the justice of God]; and their hope shall be to give up the ghost.*

How sad that day will be when people will be searching for relief and they find none. It says in scripture there will not be one drop of water in Hell. Can you imagine living eternally thirsty for just one drop of water?

We must not kid ourselves. There is a place called Hell. There will be those who were wicked who will live in Hell forever. They will not escape the justice of God.

Who do you need to share this with today?

Dear God, help me to tell others that Hell is real. Who do you need for me to show? Lord, use me to tell others that you are a God of Justice and that you desire for them to live with you. I love you Amen.

Psalm 7:17
*I will give to the Lord the thanks due to His rightness and justice, and I will sing praise to the name of the Lord Most High.*

The Lord loves it when we thank him. You know that is a characteristic we have lost today. Thank you notes are so rare today. It used to be any time you received a gift you would never forget to send a thank you note. When was the last time you sent a thank you note?

We must be a people who THANK others often, especially God. Everyday remember to thank God for all He has done for you. God loves a grateful heart!

Dear God, help me to be more thankful with others. Let this be a characteristic that shows others you are in me. Lord I thank you for all you do and help me to respond in thankfulness to you daily. I love you. Amen.

<u>Psalm 33:5</u>
*He loves righteousness and justice; the earth is full of the loving-kindness of the Lord.*

Look around the world today to find his loving-kindness. Look at the sky with the bright sun and think of his love for giving the warmth of the sun. Look at the waters rolling and thank him for drinking water. A God that Loves us and gives all we need.

The Lord is so good to us. He did not overlook one detail for us to live comfortably in the world. Do we acknowledge his loving kindness and goodness often enough? Today, look around the world and see his love and thank him for all He has done.

Dear God, I thank you for providing everything I need. Lord, help me to see you daily in the nature around me. Help me to see the purpose of all you set before me and to be more thankful for it. I love you. Amen.

Psalm 37:28
*For the Lord delights in justice and forsakes not His saints; they are preserved forever, but the offspring of the wicked [in time] shall be cut off.*

Again, we are reminded that God will cut us off eventually and forever. The good news is that God delights in us who He calls saints.

God will preserve us forever, and we will live with him eternally in heaven. God will never leave or forsake us. He promises that nothing, no sin, will ever separate us from the Love of God.

Thank you, Lord, for being a sovereign God. Thank you for being a God of Justice so that we know your laws will be realized. Lord, help me to have the confidence that you will preserve me even when life is so tough and unbearable. I know one day that I will be with you. I love you. Amen.

<u>Psalm 89:14</u>
*Righteousness and justice are the foundation of Your throne; mercy and loving-kindness and truth go before Your face.*

The foundation is what we build relationships on, buildings on, and hopes on. God's foundation is built on righteousness and justice. God's throne sits upon it.

Lord, thank you for Jesus who makes us righteous, in right standing with you. Through his blood, we are made righteous. Lord, thank you for being the God of justice. Lord, we know you will make all things right that are wrong.

Lord, I need you to be my foundation. If I make you my foundation in all that I am then I will never fall into the sea of darkness. Lord, thank you for making right the wrongs of life. Let me feel you as I stand firm today. I love you. Amen.

<u>Psalm 103:6</u>
*The Lord executes righteousness and*
*justice [not for me only, but] for all who*
*are oppressed.*

There are many who are oppressed.
Many are put down or weighted down.
You don't have to be in physical chains
to be oppressed. You may struggle with
addictions, wrong thinking, or a religious
spirit all of which is a form of oppression.

God has sent Jesus to set the oppressed
free. Go to Jesus today and tell him what is
oppressing you. Confess what is holding a
stranglehold on you. Then in the name of
Jesus and blood of Christ, ask God to bind
them off of you. Then, you will be set free.

Dear God, help me to break free from
oppression. Lord, I ask you in the name
of Jesus to bind any enemy holds on me.
Lord, I confess my sin. Thank you for
setting me free. I love you. Amen.

Psalm 140:12

*I know and rest in confidence upon it that the Lord will maintain the cause of the afflicted, and will secure justice for the poor and needy [of His believing children].*

You know many people don't understand why God allows afflictions. God is in control but He can't keep life from happening. God can't just make only good things happen because of the devil and because of man's own choice.

Today your life is full of choices that can make you a better person. Are you making healthy and wise choices? Or are you making self-defeating choices? Ask God today to help you make choices that will keep your chances of afflictions to a minimum.

Dear God, I know you are in control of everything. I know many times we suffer due to our own poor choices. Please Lord, help me to make good choices for my life. I love you. Amen.

<u>Isaiah 61:8</u>
*For I the Lord love justice;*

God will make things right. If your husband walked out on you and he never came back, God will make it right. If your son or daughter was maliciously hurt or killed, God will make it right. If you have suffered illness and despair due to someone else's bad choices, God will make it right. God is a lover of Justice.

God hates injustice. He never wants us to feel defeated. We are winners as children of God, and He will make all things right. God says, "Vengeance is mine." God will make sure justice is done.

Dear God, thank you for loving justice. Sometimes Lord, that is the only thing that keeps me going when things happen that I know are not right. Please Lord, come soon and exercise your justice. I love you. Amen.

<u>Romans 9:28</u>
*For the Lord will execute His sentence upon the earth [He will conclude and close His account with men completely and without delay], rigorously cutting it short in His justice.*

The Lord will be our judge. Again, the world wants us to believe that God will excuse our sinful living. If we go through this life sinning and failing, if we do not repent and turn our ways taking Jesus as our Savior, we will be sentenced.

The Lord will be ready on that day. It will be short as the scripture states. There will be no pleading and no second chances after death. Here me, oh friend. Wake up, repent and take Jesus into your heart today.

Lord, I know you will come to judge this earth and all that live within it. Lord, I take you in my heart, repent, and declare Jesus as my Savior. Lord, help me to show someone this today. I love you. Amen.

Revelation 19:11

*After that I saw heaven opened, and*
*behold, a white horse [appeared]! The*
*One Who was riding it is called Faithful*
*(Trustworthy, Loyal, Incorruptible, Steady)*
*and True, and He passes judgment and*
*wages war in righteousness (holiness,*
*justice, and uprightness)*

Jesus will be on a white horse coming to
get his followers on the judgment day!
Thank you, Jesus, for rescuing us.

How can we describe who Jesus is? The
words in scripture call him: Trustworthy,
Loyal, Incorruptible, Steady, and True.
WHOA! What a list to follow. Today as
you read this, ask yourself if you have
these qualities too?

Dear God, please help me to be more like
Jesus. You sent him to save the world but
also to show us how to live. Lord, help me
to be more trustworthy, loyal, true, and
steady. Lord, I desire to be more like you
today. I love you. Amen.

Job 22:21
*Acquaint now yourself with Him [agree
with God and show yourself to be
conformed to His will] and be at peace;
by that [you shall prosper and great] good
shall come to you.*

How many of you know that we must
agree with God? To agree is to have the
same views about things. Do you have the
same views as God?

Our lives must show God that we are in
agreement to what He has asked us to do.
We must not conform to this world but
conform to what God desires. The great
part of this is when we do, we will have
peace, and prosperity and goodness will
come to you.

Lord, today I want to feel you as my
soul agrees with you. I surrender any last
worldly views and ask that you give me
new eyes, just like yours. Lord, I want
what you desire, so I can prosper and have
peace. Lord, thank you for your blessings. I
love you. Amen.

Isaiah 57:21

*There is no peace, says my God, for the wicked.*

Can you imagine never having peace? Do you know people in your family or circle of friends who suffer from never feeling the peace of God? I do. My heart breaks for many because they are so wrapped up in sin they can't even get a good night's rest.

Someone asked in a talk one night, how do you sleep at night? Many said they slept OK, but many said not well at all. The speaker said you can only rest if you are in good relations with God. I think he is on to something. How can we sleep well if we are wrestling with God and sin? Are you due for a good night's rest?

Dear God, I need to rest. Lord, please help me to line up my life and forgive me of my sin. Lord, I don't to wrestle anymore. Let me feel you today as I rest like never before tonight as I sleep like a baby. I love you. Amen.

Matthew 5:9
*Blessed (enjoying enviable happiness, spiritually prosperous - with life-joy and satisfaction in God's favor and salvation, regardless of their outward conditions) are the makers and maintainers of peace, for they shall be called the sons of God!*

This shows us how little outward appearances really mean to God. The best way to put it simply, we are the hosts or keepers of the spirit that is within us. There is spirit man inside of all of us, our soul, and our flesh just houses it until the judgment day.

This doesn't mean you don't keep yourself nice and healthy, but, it also means you don't over do the outside either. We live in a society which makes us feel we must be bone thin and look young forever. When you are 60 years old, you must look 40 years old. Don't surrender to this standard. In the end, it all turns to dust.

Lord, thank you for our Holy Spirit man inside of us. Help me to be beautiful inside then out. I love you. Amen.

Romans 5:1
*Therefore, since we are justified (acquitted,
declared righteous, and given a right
standing with God) through faith, let us
[grasp the fact that we] have [the peace of
reconciliation to hold and to enjoy] peace
with God through our Lord Jesus Christ
(the Messiah, the Anointed One).*

Sometimes it is hard to feel the joy in
Christ. We get caught in all the mess the
world surrounds us in, and we forget whose
we are. We seem to just survive the day.

Today, make a point to ask God to touch
you in a way that you can hold on to peace.
Through this, your heart may can endure
and possibly enjoy today. We must hold on
to God especially in difficult times because
He is the only one who can pull us through.

Dear God, I sometimes drown in problems.
Lord, today give me your peace that I
might enjoy the day in spite of what I face.
I know, Lord, that sometimes, I must go
through hardships to get to where I need to
go. I love you. Amen.

<u>Romans 15:33</u>
*May [our] peace-giving God be with you all! Amen (so be it).*

God will give us peace. He is the only one who can provide peace in a way that we can withhold adversity. Today let us focus on God being our peace.

God, today we all need to be overwhelmed in the presence of your peace. Lord, let the world just slip away as we glide into the safety of your arms. Lord, your peace is a peace that passes all understanding. Only you God, know how much we need it and how much to give us.

Dear God, I lean on you today. I wipe away the world today and just seek your heart and your peace. Lord, just let me overflow with peace that knows all things will work out for those that love you. Lord, I do love you. Amen.

<u>Romans 16:20</u>
*And the God of peace will soon crush
Satan under your feet. The grace of our
Lord Jesus Christ (the Messiah) be with
you*

Satan, get ready; your day is coming.
For all the hell you have put us through
on earth, all the pain we have had to
overcome, Satan, you are a liar, and your
ways are cunning. But, your day is ending!

Oh Lord, I can't wait to live a day without
temptations. I can't wait not to struggle
with addictions and disappointments.
Lord, there is coming a day where you will
crush Satan, and he will be dead for your
children forever. But, oh, to those who did
not choose you Lord, they will go with
Satan forever.

Dear God, thank you for the victory we
already have. Just knowing you will crush
Satan for me gives me encouragement I
can fight another day. Lord, help me to
alert others they will be crushed too if they
don't come to you! I love you Amen.

1 Corinthians 14:33

*For He [Who is the source of their prophesying] is not a God of confusion and disorder but of peace and order.*

When I am confused about decisions, about choices, or about people in my life, I stop. Then I pray to God and ask him to make things clear. I know God is a God of order. God is not a spirit of confusion. However, the enemy loves to keep us confused.

Today, if you are making decisions, choices, or making relationship choices, feel God's presence when you stop and ask him to clear your mind and thoughts. God will give you answers that will provide clarity to what you need to know and do.

Dear God, I stop it all right now. I bow down on my knees and ask you to make order of my life. Lord, I am listening to you for guidance and clarity. I know you know best and you are a God of order and peace. I love you. Amen.

Galatians 6:16
*Peace and mercy be upon all who walk by this rule [who discipline themselves and regulate their lives by this principle], even upon the [true] Israel of God!*

Mercy, this is a word we rarely hear about anymore. It is defined as: compassionate or kindly forbearance shown toward an offender, an enemy, or other person in one's power. God knows our hearts. Therefore, if we are constantly seeking him, He shows us mercy.

Even if we fall or sin and we get back up, God extends his mercy. God knows we will never live a day without sin. But, we must confess it everyday so that God can extend his mercy and grace over our lives and walk upright through the blood of Jesus Christ.

Dear God, where would we be without your mercy? Oh Lord, thank you for looking at the intentions of our hearts and for knowing that we are trying. I love you. Amen.

Philippians 4:7
*And God's peace [shall be yours, that
tranquil state of a soul assured of its
salvation through Christ, and so fearing
nothing from God and being content with
its earthly lot of whatever sort that is, that
peace] which transcends all understanding
shall garrison and mount guard over your
hearts and minds in Christ Jesus.*

Tranquility a feeling of calm and peace, it
shall be ours knowing we are saved by the
blood of Christ. So, today when the enemy
tries to get us in a panic or tries to get
fearful, remember this scripture.

When opposed by the enemy I ask God to
give me a tranquil spirit. Ask God to lower
blood pressures, keep our mouths pure, and
to settle nerves with calmness. The enemy
will have to run and try another tactic.

Dear God, calmness does not come easy
for me. It's hard when I am rushed, mad, or
disappointed to be calm. Lord, I ask you to
give me a tranquil spirit to fight the enemy
with today. I love you. Amen.

<u>1 Peter 3:11</u>

*Let him turn away from wickedness and shun it, and let him do right. Let him search for peace (harmony; undisturbedness from fears, agitating passions, and moral conflicts) and seek it eagerly. [Do not merely desire peaceful relations with God, with your fellowmen, and with yourself, but pursue, go after them!]*

Peaceful relations with anyone can take a lot of work! That is why God says, blessed are the peacemakers for they shall inherit the Kingdom of Heaven. It's hard to remain peaceful when men are wicked. Peace does not exist with sin, and the world is so dark.

God, ask us to help others shun from wickedness. Ask a friend you know is sinning to change their life through Christ. What do we have to lose? God is waiting on us to be his peacemakers.

Dear God, help me to be a peacemaker. Lord, I find it hard to overlook the wicked ways of people, but let me be vessel of peace today so that others will see you. I love you. Amen.

<u>2 John 1:3</u>

*Grace (spiritual blessing), mercy, and
[soul] peace will be with us, from God
the Father and from Jesus Christ (the
Messiah), the Father's Son, in all sincerity
(truth) and love.*

Sincerity is another lost trait these days. It
can be defined as freedom from deceit and
hypocrisy. How many people do you know
who live as though they are free? How
many people tell you one thing and then do
another?

Look at our modern politicians. They say
they are monogamous, and then they are
found to be adulterers. Pastors judge
members who are gay, and then they are
found in homosexual activity. Sincerity has
been lost in the most Holy places, and it
makes me sick.

Dear God, please I ask you to make me
sincere today. Allow me to live free in your
victory and to be and act as to who I say I
am. Lord, let me sincere so others will see
your presence in me. I love you. Amen.

<u>Psalm 34:8</u>
*O taste and see that the Lord [our God]
is good! Blessed (happy, fortunate, to be
envied) is the man who trusts and takes
refuge in Him.*


Who ever dreamed you could taste the
Lord? Have you ever said the statement,
"That person put a bad taste in my mouth?"
I have said it, and I meant it.

Today I ask you to taste God and see that
He is good. His peace quenches a thirst like
no other. His mercy floods our hearts like a
river. His love warms our souls to the core.
Out of the abundance, our hearts speak and
taste the goodness of God!

Dear God, thank you that I can taste your
goodness. Thank you that I never walk
away with a bitter tongue. I love you so
much. Amen.

*Day 212*

<u>Proverbs 31:18</u>

*She tastes and sees that her gain from work [with and for God] is good; her lamp goes not out, but it burns on continually through the night [of trouble, privation, or sorrow, warning away fear, doubt, and distrust].*

Here this woman tastes the loyalty of God. She knows that God has been there all the while she worked. She has confidence that God will always sustain her.

Where do you need a taste of loyalty today? Where do you see loss of hope? Is it in a marriage, a child who has gone wild, or a sickness? Allow God to put a taste in your mouth today of loyalty and wash away your fears and doubt. God is a God to trust.

Dear God, I want to taste your loyalty. Lord, help me to wash down the fears and doubt over my life. Lord, you cancel all fears, sorrow, and doubt today with your presence of loyalty. I love you. Amen.

Matthew 5:13

*You are the salt of the earth, but if salt has lost its taste (its strength, its quality), how can its saltness be restored? It is not good for anything any longer but to be thrown out and trodden underfoot by men.*

One of my favorite examples of God's taste buds! God created salt to be a preserver. In those days salt was used to preserve meats so that it would be edible for long periods of time. We were made the salt of the earth ourselves in his creation.

God needed us to be the salt of the earth to preserve his goodness. How can we preserve his goodness if we no longer have salt content? We must stay strong and pure so that our salt can be used to preserve what God intends for good.

Dear God, help me to seek your strength and qualities so that my salt level stays high. Lord, I am honored you would choose me to help you preserve the goodness of the world. I love you. Amen.

<u>Mark 9:50</u>
*Salt is good (beneficial), but if salt has
lost its saltness, how will you restore [the
saltness to] it? Have salt within yourselves,
and be at peace and live in harmony with
one another.*

This is incredible thought, once the salt
loses its saltness, it can't become salty
again. God says there is a time when all
chances are over. Not because He does not
love us or want us, but life ends. Time is
up.

Today, ask God to give you a taste test.
Where are you on the salty level? Are you
staying in his word where you gain your
strength? Are you living a life that makes
salt deposits into your salt dome? Ask God
to taste you and listen to his reply.

Dear God, don't me lie to my self. Help
me to know if I am where I need to be with
you. Lord, make me the salt of the earth
and one you can count on. Lord, taste me
and tell me today what I need from you. I
love you. Amen.

Luke 14:34
*Salt is good [an excellent thing], but if salt has lost its strength and has become saltless (insipid, flat), how shall its saltness be restored?*

Salt is also used when making bread. It is needed to help make a piece of bread rise. If there is not enough salt, it can ruin the entire batch of bread.

Are you making a difference for the Kingdom at work? At play? With your family? Are you helping bring people up or down with your influence? God is counting on all of us to be his hands and feet and his salt! Are we beckoning to his call or are we living as we want to?

Dear God, help me to be a better influence on all that I am in contact with. Lord, let me be your salt that brings people higher in relationship with you. Lord, help me to do better and to live for you today and not myself. I love you. Amen.

<u>Psalm 19:10</u>
*More to be desired are they than gold, even than much fine gold; they are sweeter also than honey and drippings from the honeycomb.*

Don't you want to be sweeter than honey from a honeycomb? Don't you want all of our words and deeds to bring a sweet savor to God's mouth?

God is our bridegroom waiting on his bride.
That is why we must stay pure and holy for the day we will be joined as his bride. Let all we do bring a sweet flavor of honey to him until we meet him on that special day.

Lord, thank you that you are my bride groom forever. Thank you that you love enough me to make me your bride. Lord, let my life stay holy and pure until we meet on that special day. Lord, let me be a sweet flavor to you always. I love you. Amen.

Psalm 119:103

*How sweet are Your words to my taste, sweeter than honey to my mouth!*

How many have considered words as sweet? My teenagers today will comment to something that they really like as "sweet." I find it too funny that they are being biblical and don't even know it.

Words can be sweet or bitter. It doesn't take a brilliant mind to assess which they are. Sweet words are sweeter than honey to the mouth because they encourage the heart and soul. Bitter words can crush a heart and destroy a soul. What words are you speaking today, sweet or bitter?

Dear God, help me to speak words that are sweet. Lord, forgive all the bitter words I have spoken in the past. I repent for saying things I should not have said. Lord, help me to keep guard over my tongue so that my words will encourage and bring hope to others. May they see your presence in me. I love you. Amen.

Proverbs 16:24
*Pleasant words are as a honeycomb, sweet to the mind and healing to the body.*

Words can bring healing to the body and the heart. I have experienced this personally. I speak words of healing over my family all the time. Sweet words about Gods healing and restoring powers, and then I claim it over us in the blood of Jesus.

Thinking pure thoughts, speaking sweet words, and then believing them can bring healing and restoration to all parts of us. The heart can be healed, the body and mind restored. Today, find scriptures of healing. The Lord will touch you through your sweet declarations and bless you.

Dear God, I speak healing over my mind, body, heart, and soul. Lord, I come to you in a sweet disposition and claim healing from my words. Thank you, Lord, for touching me with your healing today. I love you. Amen.

<u>Ecclesiastes 5:12</u>
*The sleep of a laboring man is sweet,*
*whether he eats little or much, but the*
*fullness of the rich will not let him sleep.*

What this tells me that if we are doing what is right and doing a good work in life, then we will sleep sweetly. If we are constantly filling ourselves with work that benefits ourselves and filling ourselves with the world, then our sleep will not be so sweet.

You can't sleep well when you do not live like God has called you to. A hangover from the party, guilt for putting yourself first, and ignoring the needs of others will keep even the most wicked from getting a good night's sleep.

So if you need a sleep aid, check your lifestyle and see if it lines up with God.

Dear God, help me to line myself up to you. Lord, a sweet sleep given by you there can be none greater with sweet dreams. I love you. Amen.

<u>Isaiah 5:20</u>
*Woe to those who call evil good and good evil, who put darkness for light and light for darkness, who put bitter for sweet and sweet for bitter!*

Deception - that's what it all boils down to. The saying "if it sounds too good to be true it probably is too good to be true" is certainly appropriate here. This is similar to when someone entices you with a sweet savor, but you know deep inside it could be bitter.

Be careful of the lies that the enemy conceives to appear sweet but end up evil and bitter. Remind yourself, if it is too good to be true, it is probably of the enemy.

Dear God, today I need to feel your presence in discernment. Lord, I need to know what words are truly sweet and not evil. Lord, let me hear you when you tell me what I should do today. I love you. Amen.

<u>Ezekiel 3:3</u>
*And He said to me, Son of man, eat this
scroll that I give you and fill your stomach
with it. Then I ate it, and it was as sweet as
honey in my mouth.*

Have you ever eaten paper? I have, and
it is not sweet. But the words of the Lord
are sweet. They are instructions for living
successfully down here on earth. We must
live on the word of God.

Today make a commitment to read the
Bible everyday. It does not matter how
long or how much, just make time to read
from the word. It is our daily bread. It is
digested into who we are. It will be sweeter
than honey when we speak.

Dear God, I made up my mind that I will
eat your words everyday; I will read the
Bible everyday as my daily bread. Lord, I
know you will honor me in this and I will
feel your presence all around and in me. I
love you. Amen.

Revelation 10:10

*So I took the little book from the angel's
hand and ate and swallowed it; it was as
sweet as honey in my mouth, but once I had
swallowed it, my stomach was embittered.*

I love another example of angels. I am so
thankful for them. I truly feel the presence
of them especially when I call out to God
for them. Obviously, they have hands too.
This little book was taken from the angel's
hand.

God's words are sweet. They are a staple
to a believer's diet. Without the word, we
would die spiritually. Remember as we
read the word to try and digest it in our
souls so that we can speak the truth.

Dear God, thank you again for your
angels. This was the first time I realized
they too had hands. Lord, thank you for
the heavenly helpers. Lord, thank you for
your word. It is sweet and a must for our
spiritual diets. I love you. Amen.

Leviticus 4:31

*And all the fat of it he shall take away,
as the fat is taken away from off the
sacrifice of peace offerings; and the priest
shall burn it on the altar for a sweet and
satisfying fragrance to the Lord; and the
priest shall make atonement for [the man],
and he shall be forgiven.*

Nothing with God is wasted. When we
sacrifice to God, there is not part of it that
goes to waste. When there was a living
sacrifice, the priest would cut the fat away
and burn it to the Lord on the altar. This
would give off a sweet fragrance that the
Lord could smell.

The Lord God Almighty smells our
sacrifices. He smells the fragrance of fat
being burnt on the altar. Amazing that God
smells just as we do!

Dear God, I sacrifice my all to you today.
May I be a sweet fragrance to you. Lord,
forgive me of many sins. I love you. Amen.

<u>Leviticus 17:6</u>
*And the priest shall dash the blood on the altar of the Lord at the door of the Tent of Meeting and burn the fat for a sweet and satisfying fragrance to the Lord.*

Nothing satisfies the Lord more than when we offer him our first fruits. That means when we give him back the gifts He gave to us such like the gift of our singing or when we give him back the first fruits of our labor. When we make money we must give him the first part of it.

Just as the burning fat at the altar, God smells our sacrifices. The Lord considers us a sweet fragrance and aroma.

Dear God, I give you my gifts to use as you need for the Kingdom. Lord, I give you my first fruits of my labor. Lord, I pray that I am a sweet smell to you as I put you first on all that I have. I love you. Amen.

Leviticus 26:31
*I will lay your cities waste, bring your sanctuaries to desolation, and I will not smell the fragrance of your sweet and soothing odors [of offerings made by fire].*

To prove that God smells like we do, He tells the sinners He will not smell their offerings. He will make the city waste smell. He will bring desolation to their sanctuaries too. But, He will not smell the soothing odors of their sacrifices because they are not for the right reasons.

Are we guilty of doing things for God just for show? Are we doing good deeds with pure intentions? If so, God will not even look your way. God will not be fooled because He looks at the heart and intentions.

Dear God, please know my intentions are pure. Lord, please let me be a sweet odor to you today. Lord, my sacrifice of praise offer a soothing fragrance. I love you. Amen.

<u>Numbers 15:13</u>
*All who are native-born shall do these
things in this way in bringing an offering
made by fire of a sweet and pleasant odor
to the Lord.*

This scripture says all who are native-born
which can be defined as belonging to a
person by birth or to a thing by nature. We
are all born into God's world. We are his
children. God breathed the breath of life
into our lungs in order that we may live.

Are we making our lives a living sacrifice
for our Father? Are we bringing the
offering of our lives to him and burning
off the fleshly desires? Are we a pleasant
and sweet odor to the Lord our Father and
King?

Dear God, today I want to feel your
presence as I leave my life at the altar.
Lord, I ask you to burn off anything that is
not of you and let me be a sweet fragrance
to you. Let my life be a pleasant odor
before you. I love you. Amen.

Numbers 28:2
*Command the Israelites, saying, My offering, My food for My offerings made by fire, My sweet and soothing odor you shall be careful to offer to Me at its proper time.*

We must go before the Lord often as a living sacrifice. This enables us to grow closer and stronger for the Lord. It will burn off more and more of the world's influence and fleshly desires. Then, as the fire refines us, we look and act more and more like our heavenly Father.

I challenge you to make an altar in your mind in your quiet time today. Ask God to burn off your worries, your pain, and the things that are keeping you from being more like him. Then, thank him that you are a sweet fragrance to him because of his love for you.

Dear God, I know the fire can be painful at the altar, but I want to be more like you. I want you to refine me by fire so that I can be a purer vessel. I love you. Amen.

Numbers 28:27

*But you shall offer the burnt offering for a sweet, pleasing, and soothing fragrance to the Lord:*

In this, we see that it is not a choice when you are a follower of God, whether or not you will or will not offer some kind of sacrifice to God. We are all called to be living sacrifices for him.

How do we do this? How do we become a sacrifice to God? Daily we must submit our will, our desires, and our plans to God's will. This is a sacrifice of who we are, and we surrender to what God wants for us.

Dear Father, today I surrender. I give you all that I am. I know I do not deserve all that you have done for me, but all I want is to be a sweet soothing fragrance to you. Lord, forgive me, and I give you all that I am today. I love you. Amen.

<u>Proverbs 27:9</u>
*Oil and perfume rejoice the heart; so does
the sweetness of a friend's counsel that
comes from the heart.*

What would we do without a few friends
on earth? Notice I said a few. I have found
out the hard way that if you can call on two
people who will be there for you no matter
what, this is a blessing. So many people
we call friends are really just what I call
"acquaintances."

Today as you feel God's presence thank
him for the one or two people in your life
who you can count on. Thank him that they
would be there at two in the morning or at
the lowest point of your life. Then thank
Jesus for being there all the time as a best
friend just waiting on you to call upon him.

Dear God, thank you for my friends today.
Thank you that I can call on at least one
person today. Lord, thank you for the
loving relationship you established for
Jesus to be called our friend as well as our
Savior. I love you. Amen.

<u>Mark 16:1</u>
*And when the Sabbath was past [that is,
after the sun had set], Mary Magdalene,
and Mary [the mother] of James, and
Salome purchased sweet-smelling spices,
so that they might go and anoint [Jesus'
body].*

Mary Magdalene and Mary knew the
stench of death would soon be setting in, so
they went and bought the sweet-smelling
spices for Jesus' body. They were going to
anoint his body with oil until He was raised
into the heavens.

The love these followers of Jesus had for
him! They went to great lengths to make
sure all was done right for him. Their love
for him was more than words. They acted
out their love for him on every level.

Dear God, let my words not be empty when
I tell you I love you. When I feel your
presence today in my heart, let my love for
you be followed by actions. Let my life
be full of ways in which I demonstrate my
love for you. I love you. Amen.

<u>2 Corinthians 2:15</u>
*For we are the sweet fragrance of Christ
[which exhales] unto God, [discernible
alike] among those who are being saved
and among those who are perishing:*

Incredible! The Lord may just be able to
sit with his eyes closed, inhale, exhale,
and know who is being saved. Again I
am shocked by the revelation that God's
physical characteristics are so much like
ours. God actually smells, inhales, and
exhales.

The Lord really smells us too! The way
to smell sweet to God is to be obedient.
Today, just give your life over to him and
ask him to take over so that you can be a
sweet fragrance for him to smell and enjoy.

Dear God, I am still amazed at how we
are so much like you in so many ways.
Sometimes because you are so holy I forget
you smell and breathe. Lord, as I feel you
today let me be a sweet fragrance for your
nose to smell today. I love you. Amen.

<u>Ephesians 5:2</u>
*And walk in love, [esteeming and delighting in one another] as Christ loved us and gave Himself up for us, a slain offering and sacrifice to God [for you, so that it became] a sweet fragrance.*

As we see in this scripture today, another way to be a sweet fragrance unto God is to love one another. Why does the enemy make this so hard to do? The enemy knows that one of the best ways to ruin a person's testimony is by offending someone. Then the world looks at the so-called Christian and says, "If that is what Christianity is all about, I don't want any part of it."

Have you made a friend in Christ angry? Have you left someone unforgiving? Don't let the enemy ruin your testimony by keeping you in bondage. Just walk in love, forgive others, and build each other up, and you will be a sweet fragrance to God.

Dear God, help me to walk in love. I want to be a sweet fragrance to you. I love you. Amen.

2 Corinthians 2:14

*But thanks be to God, Who in Christ always leads us in triumph [as trophies of Christ's victory] and through us spreads and makes evident the fragrance of the knowledge of God everywhere,*

In this scripture, we see that knowledge has a fragrance too. Fragrance can be defined as atmosphere and a distinctive and pervasive quality or character. So through our knowledge of God, we create an atmosphere or persuasive quality that is seen and smelled everywhere.

Haven't you experienced this before, someone you know is Godly by the way they have given their lives to Christ just exudes an aura of knowledge, love, and sweetness? This needs to be a goal for us too.

Dear God, please let me have the fragrance of your knowledge. Let me be a sweet influence on all those everywhere. Lord, thank you for loving me. I love you. Amen.

2 Corinthians 2:15

*For we are the sweet fragrance of Christ [which exhales] unto God, [discernible alike] among those who are being saved and among those who are perishing:*

I get compliments all the time on a certain fragrance of perfume I wear. I can be at a grocery store, restaurant, or working, and I will have people stop me to ask me what fragrance I am wearing. Now, I give God all the glory about the way I smell and say it is the fragrance of Jesus in my soul.

God will smell our sweet fragrance us as He saves us from eternal death. Jesus will cover us with his blood, and He will give us a beautiful aroma to our Father. What a beautiful image as we pass before the Lord, and He delights in the sweet fragrance of our existence.

Dear Lord, I long to be a sweet fragrance for you. Lord, let me feel your presence today as I emit a sweet fragrance of obedience and love to you. I love you. Amen.

## 2 Corinthians 2:16

*To the latter it is an aroma [wafted] from death to death [a fatal odor, the smell of doom]; to the former it is an aroma from life to life [a vital fragrance, living and fresh]. And who is qualified (fit and sufficient) for these things? [Who is able for such a ministry? We?]*

Do we witness to the world that is wafting in death? Do we tolerate the aroma of death and sin that surrounds us when we know better? Do we share with others the doom which is in store for them unless they confess that Jesus is the Lord and Savior and repent?

We must offer to all a fresh fragrance! We must help people to find victory in Jesus. We are able. God is counting on all of us!

Dear God, please forgive me when I don't share who you are with those who are living in sin and death. Lord, as I feel you today, fill me with your sweet fragrance and give me courage to share the life of victory in Christ with all I see. I love you. Amen.

Genesis 8:21

*When the Lord smelled the pleasing odor [a scent of satisfaction to His heart], the Lord said to Himself, I will never again curse the ground because of man, for the imagination (the strong desire) of man's heart is evil and wicked from his youth; neither will I ever again smite and destroy every living thing, as I have done.*

God finds every way to redeem our sins. The Lord just looks for a few who will be pleasing to him. Through these people God shows mercy and grace to all.

God never intended for man to perish. God never intended bad things to happen here on earth. But through our own sins and arrogance, God has allowed us to have sin in our lives. However, God never leaves us or gives up on us. God is always here and loves us.

Dear God, I know you don't wish the evil of the world on us. I know you love me. Lord, thank you for not cursing man forever. I want to satisfy you and be a sweet smell to you. I love you. Amen.

<u>Deuteronomy 28:1</u>
*If you will listen diligently to the voice of
the Lord your God, being watchful to do all
His commandments which I command you
this day, the Lord your God will set you
high above all the nations of the earth.*

Do you hear God? Some ask me," How do
you hear God?" It's a very simple answer. If
you feel a need to call someone, stop to help
someone, or see a different option no one
sees, that is God speaking to you.

God will use so many ways to get to you.
God uses the Bible, his own words, if you
will read them. God will use a friend to
affirm something you already thought of.
God will use even a billboard to open your
ears and heart.

Today Lord, I want to hear you. Open my
ears and heart to allow you to get to me.
I will be more aware of what my heart is
nudging for me to do. Then, Lord, I will
wait to hear you. I love you. Amen.

<u>Judges 13:9</u>
*And God listened to the voice of Manoah,
and the Angel of God came again to the
woman as she sat in the field; but Manoah
her husband was not with her.*

I love when the scriptures describes God
so vividly and simply. God listened. This
is so reassuring to me some days when all
Hell seems to be around me. Then, my only
option on these days is to cry out to God.

God listens. All I have to do is say those
two words and know that God knows my
pain. I know He hears my heart cry to him.
Today, as you search to feel him, know He
hears you.

Dear God, thank you for the scriptures as
simple as this one, "God listens." What a
reassuring fact to quote when my life is
falling apart. I cry to you today and know
that you hear me. I love you. Amen.

Psalm 4:3
*But know that the Lord has set apart for
Himself [and given distinction to] him who
is godly [the man of loving-kindness]. The
Lord listens and heeds when I call to Him.*

I tell my children all the time that to be
a Christ follower you will have to set
yourself apart from this world. I don't
mean in an arrogant way. I mean you will
have to act and react differently to what the
world says and does as a child of God.

Just having the characteristic of being
loving sets you apart in God's eyes. It is
amazing to me that the world is so full of
hate and selfishness. For those who live
lovingly, God hears them and sets them
apart.

Dear God, help me to be more loving like
you. Lord, I know that just loving people
sets me apart from most. Lord, I want you
to hear me, and I know you will heed my
call because I love as you commanded. I
love you. Amen.

<u>Psalm 85:8</u>
*I will listen [with expectancy] to what God the Lord will say, for He will speak peace to His people, to His saints (those who are in right standing with Him) - but let them not turn again to [self-confident] folly.*

I love to wait for God expectantly. I loved when I was nine months pregnant. Expecting a child was so exciting knowing that at any moment I could go into labor. This is a great trait to incorporate into our everyday lives, expectancy!

What are you expecting God to do for you today? What do you need him to do for you today? Expect what you need! Listen, wait, and expect God today.

Dear God, I am now living everyday with expectancy. I expect to feel you, hear you, and have what you promised I would. Thank you for never letting us down. You are a God that never fails. I love you. Amen.

Jeremiah 7:23
*But this thing I did command them: Listen
to and obey My voice, and I will be your
God and you will be My people; and walk
in the whole way that I command you, that
it may be well with you.*

All we have to do is listen to God. To
listen means that all you have to do is read
his word, the Bible. That is listening. Then
you must be doers of the word. This means
to walk in the whole way that God asks us
to do in scriptures.

Another great bonus from reading the word
is your faith builds and builds. Faith comes
by hearing the word. So as you read the
word, your faith builds, and your actions
become obedient to what you are reading
and being told to do by God.

Dear God, thank you for the breath inspired
words of the Bible. Thank you that you
speak to all of us through the scriptures.
Then, Lord, you bless us by building our
faith and making our walk whole. I love
you. Amen.

Jeremiah 11:4

*Which I commanded your fathers at the
time that I brought them out of the land of
Egypt, from the iron furnace, saying, Listen
to My voice and do according to all that I
command you. So will you be My people,
and I will be your God,*

God reminds us here of what He has
brought us out of. God has brought us out
of deaths' gloom, out Hell. God has given
us life through his Son Jesus Christ.

It is nice to remind ourselves what trials
God has brought us out of in our present
lives. He brought my dying marriage life.
He brought my sinful Soul life through the
blood of Jesus. What has God brought you
through in your life?

Dear God, I feel you today through the
power of restoration. Thank you for the
times you have rescued me. Thank you
that you instruct us not only to remind
ourselves but also to remind you of what
you have done for us have promised for us.
I love you. Amen.

<u>Hosea 9:17</u>
*My God will cast them away because they did not listen to and obey Him, and they shall be wanderers and fugitives among the nations.*

Do you want to be a castaway? Can you imagine being on the end of a fishing pole being cast away forever to sit alone? I can't imagine what that would be like.

God will cast those away who do not listen. They will have to wander through life and be lost. They will not belong as a citizen of heaven.

Today, make a commitment to take a few minutes each day just to sit and listen for God. Ask God to tell you one thing in that few minutes; He will.

Dear God, thank you for your presence today. I hear you, and I thank you. Lord, thank you that I am not a cast away. Lord, help me to harvest sinners for you so they may hear you too. I love you. Amen.

Matthew 13:43
*Then will the righteous (those who are upright and in right standing with God) shine forth like the sun in the kingdom of their Father. Let him who has ears [to hear] be listening, and let him consider and perceive and understand by hearing.*

Today we need to ask Lord that when we hear him speak that we understand him too. Many times, I have heard God speak but I did not get the revelation of what I was to do with what I was hearing.

Ask the Lord to give you instructions when you hear him speak. Let God show us what He needs us to do. We want to shine like the sun so that the world will see that we do indeed hear and understand God.

Dear God, I hear you today and Lord, show me your presence by helping me to understand what you need me to do. Lord, thank you that I will shine to the world for your glory in order to help others hear you. I love you. Amen.

John 8:47

*Whoever is of God listens to God. [Those who belong to God hear the words of God.] This is the reason that you do not listen [to those words, to Me]: because you do not belong to God and are not of God or in harmony with Him.*

As we see here today that whoever is of God will hear him. Don't let the enemy tell you any more lies about hearing God. Right here it plainly states that whoever is of God will listen and hear him.

The enemy loves to lie and tell you that was in Biblical times only. WRONG! God speaks to us everyday. Listen for his words. Start by reading his words in the bible. You will be amazed how much you will hear!

Dear God, don't let me fall for the enemy lies that I can't hear you. Lord, let me feel you today as I pray and read your words that I will hear you speak. I love you. Amen.

John 9:31

*We know that God does not listen to sinners; but if anyone is God-fearing and a worshiper of Him and does His will, He listens to him.*

We see it everyday, people drowning in their own consequences of sin. Many people do not have a clue that all of their messes could be cleaned up with one simple solution, Jesus.

God knows we are sinners. However, what separates us as Christ followers who are also sinners is that we carry a reverent fear of God. We ask for forgiveness and healing. We don't continue to sin and not fear God. Ask yourself today, do I fear God, as I should? Then ask God to show you what reverential fear is to him.

Dear God, I want to feel you presence today in the healthy fear of you I should possess. Lord, help me to sin less and forgive me of failing you. Lord, I worship you and I want to reverently fear you and listen to you. I love you. Amen.

<u>1 John 4:6</u>
*We are [children] of God. Whoever is
learning to know God [progressively to
perceive, recognize, and understand God
by observation and experience, and to get
an ever-clearer knowledge of Him] listens
to us; and he who is not of God does not
listen or pay attention to us. By this we
know (recognize) the Spirit of Truth and
the spirit of error.*

Knowing God is a learning process. We
don't just wake up one day and know
all about what God is and who He is.
Personally, the best way I have grown in
the knowledge of God is by falling, failing,
and experiencing his love and redemption.
Then I learned more about God by the
power of him moving through me to
accomplish his purpose for my life.

Dear God, in your presence right now I
want to feel your redemption. Lord, just let
your mercy and grace overflow my heart.
Lord, I want to learn more about you so
that I can be more like you. I want to live
in the Spirit and truth. I love you. Amen.

Revelation 2:7

*He who is able to hear, let him listen to and give heed to what the Spirit says to the assemblies (churches). To him who overcomes (is victorious), I will grant to eat [of the fruit] of the tree of life, which is in the paradise of God.*

Sometimes I am not sure the churches are listening to God. They may appear to be a church that listens but I am learning to really question many churches. Lately I feel strongly that churches have forgotten the sheep that God has called us to save.

My entire life is centered on this one move of God. God says that there will be more celebrating for the one sheep that is found and brought back to him than the 99 that don't need him. My life is now focused on the one. I wonder if the churches are too caught up in building funds, salaries, and keeping members so no one else gets them that they missed hearing God on this!

Dear God, be with the churches. We are the church too. I love you. Amen.

Revelation 22:18

*I [personally solemnly] warn everyone who
listens to the statements of the prophecy
[the predictions and the consolations and
admonitions pertaining to them] in this
book: If anyone shall add anything to them,
God will add and lay upon him the plagues
(the afflictions and the calamities) that are
recorded and described in this book.*

WHOA! This is powerful. Let no man
take away or add to what God has breathed
into scriptures. Be on guard to those that
say thus saith the Lord and speak outside
of scriptures. God will pay them back with
afflictions and calamities forever.

Dear God, help me to say only what is in
the Bible. Let my words be guarded and
few. Lord, let my heart discern whom I
should believe when they speak in your
name. In your presence Lord, today I ask
that I not be deceived from anyone who is
not of you.  I love you. Amen.

<u>Proverbs 4:22</u>
*For they are life to those who find them,*
*healing and health to all their flesh.*

The scriptures before this say, "My son, pay attention to what I say; listen closely to my words. Do not let them out of your sight; keep them within your heart." The words God gives us in scriptures are LIFE to those that find them. The word is the only place to find life, healing, and health.

If you need healing today then go to the word. Find all the scriptures on restoration and healing. Then, claim them for your life everyday. Say them over your life everyday. The, healing and health will manifest in your life through the power of the words of God.

Dear God, help me to stay in your word. Lord, help me to find the scriptures I need to speak over my life. Lord, let me feel your presence in the manifestation of healing today. I love you. Amen.

<u>Isaiah 58:8</u>
*Then shall your light break forth like
the morning, and your healing (your
restoration and the power of a new
life) shall spring forth speedily; your
righteousness (your rightness, your justice,
and your right relationship with God) shall
go before you [conducting you to peace
and prosperity], and the glory of the Lord
shall be your rear guard.*

Until I was in the midst writing this book
had I never seen this fact, the Lord shall
be your rear guard." This spoke volumes
to me on a deep personal level because
one of my biggest weaknesses to date is
not having the faith that God has my back.
If this scripture was written in today's
language it would read, don't worry, God
has your back.

Oh Lord, today let me feel you in the
assurance that you do have my back. Don't
let me fall into the familiar trap the enemy
sets for me in not trusting you completely. I
love you. Amen.

Jeremiah 33:6
*Behold, [in the future restored Jerusalem]*
*I will lay upon it health and healing, and I*
*will cure them and will reveal to them the*
*abundance of peace (prosperity, security,*
*stability) and truth*

Sometimes people look for cures in the
wrong ways. Sometimes a cure doesn't
come in a physical manifestation. God says
here that healing and cures can come in the
forms of peace, truth, prosperity, stability,
security, and truth.

I could sure use healing in all of these
areas. How about you? Does your life need
more peace, prosperity, security, stability,
and truth? Ask God to show up today in
one of these areas in your life.

Dear God, I need all of the above. I need
peace mostly and then security. Lord,
please let me feel you today through a
peace that passes all understanding and in
the assurance, you are with me. I love you.
Amen.

<u>Matthew 4:23</u>
*And He went about all Galilee, teaching in
their synagogues and preaching the good
news (Gospel) of the kingdom, and healing
every disease and every weakness and
infirmity among the people.*

What a great word for all of us today! That
Jesus healed every disease. Not just some
diseases were healed, BUT all diseases
were healed by Jesus. Remember that Jesus
is the same yesterday, today and tomorrow,
a God that doesn't change.

What disease do you need healing from
today? Do you have alcoholism, heart
disease, diabetes, cancer, or a disease
of the mind such as worry, anxiety, and
depression? Jesus came and died so that we
could be healed from ALL diseases.

Dear God, I ask today for healing. I need
your presence manifested in taking away
addictions, worry, and anxiety today. Lord,
let my heart be receptive that you do still
heal today. I love you. Amen.

<u>Matthew 8:4</u>
*And Jesus said to him, See that you tell
nothing about this to anyone; but go,
show yourself to the priest and present
the offering that Moses commanded, for
a testimony [to your healing] and as an
evidence to the people.*

Sometimes it is best not to share your
glory news right away. I think God wants
others to notice it first. Then they can open
their hearts for the answer.

Today, I ask God to open the hearts of
some of my inner circle, so they can see
God, not me, in what is happening in my
life. It is so hard some days to keep it quiet.
But God will make the opportunity happen
at the perfect time for me to share my God
news in my life.

Dear God, I know you work on hearts all
the time. Lord, open the hearts of some so
that they can see your mighty works in my
life. Lord, let me be aware of your timing
because it is always perfect. I love you.
Amen.

<u>Matthew 11:5</u>
*The blind receive their sight and the lame*
*walk, lepers are cleansed (by healing)*
*and the deaf hear, the dead are raised up*
*and the poor have good news (the Gospel)*
*preached to them.*

This is not only good news, but it is great news! God can make the blind see, the lame walk, the deaf hear, the dead will be raised, and the poor will be taken care of. Don't let the enemy stifle your faith on this fact of healing. Remember God is the same yesterday, today, and tomorrow - a God that does not change.

Ask God to heal you. Ask God to heal someone dear to you. Activate your faith today by decreeing and believing it. It will be done.

Dear God, forgive my disbelief. Forgive me when I fail to believe completely that you do heal today. Lord, heal me and my loved one. I will decree this over my life and activate my faith in you. I love you. Amen.

Luke 5:14

*And [Jesus] charged him to tell no one
[that he might chance to meet], until
[He said] you go and show yourself to
the priest, and make an offering for your
purification, as Moses commanded, for a
testimony and proof to the people, that they
may have evidence [of your healing].*

Sometimes healing comes with a
contingency. God will give us instructions,
and unless we do exactly what He asks
of us, then He will not follow through
with it. Make sure as you ask for healing,
that when God speaks to you, that you do
exactly as He says.

Don't try to fabricate or manipulate God.
God does not work under these conditions.
Just pray, ask, and obey, and God will
deliver you.

Dear God, help me to hear you and do
exactly what I must do. Lord, let me not try
and rush anything, help me to be patient
and obedient. I love you. Amen.

<u>Luke 6:19</u>
*And all the multitude were seeking to touch
Him, for healing power was all the while
going forth from Him and curing them
all [saving them from severe illnesses or
calamities].*

Amazing that Jesus was healing and curing
all kinds of people by just a touch! Then
the healings were just pouring out just
from his presence. I pray for this anointing
for all of us. I pray that the Jesus who lived
and performed these miracles will choose
some of us to be the vessels for these
miracles.

I have been blessed to lay my hands on
my own husband, and God honored us by
healing him. Healing is real and available.
God is no respecter of persons. All that you
need is faith that God can do it! Remember
we serve the God who does the impossible!

Dear God, again I ask you to raise my faith
in healing. Lord, let me feel your presence
today as I pray for healing and allow me to
see the manifestation. I love you. Amen.

Luke 7:21
*In that very hour Jesus was healing many
[people] of sicknesses and distressing
bodily plagues and evil spirits, and to
many who were blind He gave [a free,
gracious, joy-giving gift of] sight.*

In this scripture, we see that evil spirits do
reside in people. I see it every day. Many
times when I minister to people I tell them
they are not fighting with the person in
front of them, they are fighting an evil
spirit inside that person.

Today if you have a disagreement,
remember you are fighting the spirit in
them. I am not saying they are possessed,
but I am saying that evil can be fought
easier when you look at the spirit in the
person in whom it lives.

Dear God, forgive me for fighting. Lord,
help me to see the enemy trying to ruin me
by fighting against me. Lord, you are my
defender and I am victorious through the
blood of Christ. I love you. Amen.

<u>Luke 9:2</u>
*And He sent them out to announce and preach the kingdom of God and to bring healing.*

All of us can heal others. All followers of Christ can go out to the world and heal others. There is a religious spirit that tries to tell us we must have some accreditation to be a vessel of healing for God. This is a lie straight from HELL.

If you are a Christ follower your prayers, your touch, and your belief can bring extraordinary results. You can bring about supernatural events. All you have to do is believe and to act on the need when it comes to your attention.

Dear God, thank you for the power of healing. Lord, help me to destroy the religious spirit that tells us we have to do something special to be a vessel for healing. Lord, use me, an ordinary person to bring about an extraordinary result. I love you. Amen.

<u>Acts 4:22</u>
*For the man on whom this sign (miracle) of healing was performed was more than forty years old.*

Here is another example of healing in scripture for us to believe. I tell you we must believe in healing. How can we go through this life without the hope that God cures and heals?

My family has experienced healing and cures. God desires all of us to live in healing. WE must believe it. Start today confessing the need for belief of God's supernatural powers in your life. Then gather all the scriptures you can on healing and know them by heart. Then your faith will be strengthened, and your hope will be increased for healing.

Dear God, help me to connect with you and your ability to heal. Lord, I want to believe it. Lord, I know you are the same forever, and you can still heal. I love you. Amen.

<u>1 Corinthians 12:9</u>
*To another [wonder-working] faith by the same [Holy] Spirit, to another the extraordinary powers of healing by the one Spirit;*

Here we see the power of coupling our faith to the extraordinary powers of God. In order to get the supernatural results, you must have both of these.

The Holy Spirit lives within us. All we have to do is believe that the power of God lives within us. Then we must call upon our inner strength powered by God and believe through our faith we can do all things through the blood of Christ.

Dear God, today I feel your presence in the knowledge I do have your power inside of me. Help me to call upon this inner man more often. Lord, show up on a small scale through my prayers, so that my faith can be built up. Lord, I love you. Amen.

<u>1 Chronicles 16:27</u>
*Honor and majesty are [found] in His presence; strength and joy are [found] in His sanctuary.*

We must honor God. When we are in his presence, not only honor should be present but majesty as well. Majesty can be defined as supreme greatness or authority; sovereignty.

Today when we are in our quiet time before God, we must come in honor and majesty before him. The, we will be rewarded with joy and strength by God.

Dear God, today I honor you with my life. Honor can be defined as putting first. Lord, I put you first in my life. I will acknowledge your infinite power and greatness. Lord, I will feel your presence when the joy and strength of your love overflow my soul today. I love you. Amen.

<u>1 Chronicles 16:33</u>
*Then shall the trees of the wood sing out for joy before the Lord, for He comes to judge and govern the earth.*

The Lord does govern the earth. Many people have lost the hope that God truly is in control of all that happens to us. The Lord must be in control, so that when He does come to judge all of us, He will have all the knowledge of what has happened.

Many of us today are struggling. It seems the world is really out of control and chaotic. It seems very dark, and fear looms everywhere. Today feel God's presence in your spirit when your heart is able to rest in the fact God truly is in control. Remember today, that we have been given full authority over the devil here on earth. Now act as if you have victory over darkness.

Dear God, thank you for being in control. Forgive me Father, that I sometimes get scared when the world looks so out of control. Lord, thank you for giving me full authority over darkness. I love you, Amen.

Nehemiah 8:10

*Then [Ezra] told them, Go your way, eat
the fat, drink the sweet drink, and send
portions to him for whom nothing is
prepared; for this day is holy to our Lord.
And be not grieved and depressed, for
the joy of the Lord is your strength and
stronghold.*

The personal revelation I received from this
is that when we do for others we will find
real joy. It's OK to fill our own needs, but
we must think of others and do for them.

The world tells us that if we have all of these
things we will be happy. However, unless
you give of yourself then you will never find
true happiness. If you are grieved or
depressed, do something for someone else
and you will surely feel the presence of God.

Dear God, thank you for all that you have
blessed me with. Please help me not miss
you by not helping others out. Then Lord, I
know you will give me joy which is where
I get my strength. Help me to help others to
be an example of you. I love you. Amen.

Job 8:21
*He will yet fill your mouth with laughter*
*[Job] and your lips with joyful shouting.*

What I love is the scripture that follows
and it says, "Your enemies will be clothed
in shame, and the tents of the wicked will
be no more." This is a great nugget of
knowledge for me. Knowing this does allow
me to laugh, and it helps me not to get so
caught up when the enemy attacks me.

Today when you are hurt by people in
your life just know that God will put them
to shame, and they will not be able to be
wicked one day. Ask God to help you feel
his presence to day by laughing and feeling
joy.

Dear God, please help me not to get so
upset and down when others hurt me. Lord,
help me put a smile on my face today in the
hopes that you will take care of my enemies.
I love you. Amen.

<u>Job 33:26</u>
*He prays to God, and He is favorable to him, so that he sees His face with joy; for [God] restores to him his righteousness (his uprightness and right standing with God - with its joys).*

Even when Job was so persecuted by the enemy and tortured, he continued to lift prayers to God. God found so much favor for his servant Job in his faithfulness of prayer even in the darkest hour of Job's life.

My question for all of us is, "Do we remain faithful and believe our prayers in our darkest hour?" I know at times I have gotten so down I even gave up on praying. Today I challenge all of us to go to God first when we are in the fight of our life and feel his presence by his favor.

Dear God, forgive me for giving up in the past. Lord, today I ask you to hear my prayers and answer them so I can find favor in your eyes. I love you. Amen.

<u>Job 36:11</u>
*If they obey and serve Him, they shall
spend their days in prosperity and their
years in pleasantness and joy.*

It really is that simple, obey, and
serve God. If we will do this then God
will give us prosperity, joy, and years
of pleasantness. We try to make our
relationship with God so complicated.

Today ask God to help you to be more
obedient to him. Ask God where He needs
you to serve for him. How can we be
his hands and feet here on earth? Then
God will be able to give us more than we
deserve.

Dear God, I want to be obedient to what
you have called me to do. Lord, help me
to serve others in a way that they see you
through me. Lord, thank you for giving me
all I need, as I desire to do what you need
from me. I love you. Amen.

Psalm 5:11

*But let all those who take refuge and put their trust in You rejoice; let them ever sing and shout for joy, because You make a covering over them and defend them; let those also who love Your name be joyful in You and be in high spirits.*

There is no refuge like God's refuge. Nothing can touch you in God's refuge. If you can trust him enough to take complete care of us, you will be able to rejoice in him.

How can others see God in us if we don't smile and show joy? How would we be set apart from most of the world if we never smiled? The best way to rejoice and have joy is to trust in the Lord with all your heart and take refuge in him today.

Dear God, help me to trust you to be my refuge. Lord, I want to be set apart from the world by just a simple smile. Lord, let the joy of your love overflow me, so the world will see you in me. I love you. Amen.

<u>Psalm 16:11</u>
*You will show me the path of life; in Your
presence is fullness of joy, at Your right
hand there are pleasures forevermore.*

Isn't this great to know that God will show
us the path of life? It takes me back to
Psalms 40 which I live by daily that God
establishes my steps, which means He
knows which steps I need to take and helps
me walk in them.

God will show us where we need to go.
If we seek his presence, He will give us
direction and joy. God desires to give us
the desires of our hearts.

Dear God, thank you for loving me so
much that you show me the steps of life.
Thank you for establishing the steps I need
to take. Lord, today I will feel the presence
of your joy because you love me and will
show me the steps I need to take. I love
you. Amen.

<u>Psalm 30:5</u>
*For His anger is but for a moment, but His favor is for a lifetime or in His favor is life. Weeping may endure for a night, but joy comes in the morning.*

These are just great scriptures to say daily. God does get mad at us but just for a moment. His love for us is forever. Therefore his favor is for a lifetime. Most importantly, weeping and pain may last longer than you want, but God will give you joy.

The enemy uses our sin to keep us in self-condemnation. The enemy attacks us most when we are down and in trials. But today, know in your heart God loves you and can't stay mad at you. If you can press through the trial, joy will be given to you by God.

Dear God, thank you for today. I will feel you as my heart receives your forgiveness and favor. Lord, I will seek your joy even in trials. I love you. Amen.

<u>Psalm 35:9</u>
*Then I shall be joyful in the Lord; I shall rejoice in His deliverance.*

God does deliver. This could mean He rescues you from a bad relationship or makes you well from sickness. God delivers today just as He did in the Bible.

I was delivered from a nicotine addiction. Many times, I tried to quit in all kinds of ways. In the end, I just surrendered through a process of feeling the reasons why I smoked in the first place. I smoked to cover hurts and pains and to prove something I was not. It was a supernatural experience with God, but I was delivered.

Dear God, thank you for delivering us today. Search me oh Lord, and see if there is any place in me I need deliverance. Is it a religious spirit, an addiction, a hardened heart, or foul tongue? Please Lord, through the blood of Christ deliver me and help me to be what you desire for me. I love you. Amen.

Psalm 71:23
*My lips shall shout for joy when I sing praises to You, and my inner being, which You have redeemed.*

Until we recognize what lives in us we will never know complete joy. We can never attain complete joy without the power of the Holy Spirit. In Timothy, it states one of the signs of the last days will be when we deny the Holy Spirit and the powers of the Holy Spirit.

Today recognize who lives in you. God lives in you. God put the Holy Spirit in us when we became followers of Christ. God equipped us with the power of the Holy Spirit, so we could experience the supernatural presence of God on demand daily.

Dear God, thank you for the Holy Spirit. Lord, help me to call upon my inner being more and to recognize that in fact it is you living in me. I love you. Amen.

<u>Psalm 95:2</u>
*Let us come before His presence with
thanksgiving; let us make a joyful noise to
Him with songs of praise!*

One sure way to get in the immediate
presence of God is with Thanksgiving. God
loves a grateful heart. God loves it when
we thank him for all that He does for us.

It is so easy to incorporate this in our daily
lives. When you first wake up thank God
for today and for allowing you to live
another day. Every time you eat thank him
for your food. Thank him all day long, and
the presence of God will devour you!

Dear God, forgive me for not being
grateful all the time. Lord, forgive me
for overlooking all that you do for me
everyday. Lord I long to be in your
presence so I will thank you more
everyday. I love you. Amen.

*Day 274*

Psalm 126:5
*They who sow in tears shall reap in joy and singing.*

This is a main principle of God, you reap what you sow. God's compassion is so overwhelming He assures us that when we cry we will reap joy one day in singing.

My question for us today is, "What are we sowing for God today in order to reap the benefits?" Try very hard to sow seeds of mercy, grace, love, and hope then you will harvest these things for your selves. It's as simple as when you plant a corn seed, you will reap an ear of corn not an apple.

Dear God, in my pain and many tears it is so comforting to know you will help me harvest or reap joy soon. Lord, just to know your compassion flows for me today helps me to feel the presence of release and rest. I love you. Amen.

<u>Proverbs 3:33</u>
*The curse of the Lord is in and on the house of the wicked, but He declares blessed (joyful and favored with blessings) the home of the just and consistently righteous.*

The word that sticks out to me today is "consistently' which can be defined as normally, regularly, customarily, routinely, and habitually. So I put this sequence of questions together for us to think about.

Do I normally pray? Do I regularly read the word of God? Do I customarily ask God first before making a decision? Do I routinely make time for God everyday? Do I habitually find ways to share the Love of God to others?

Dear God, today I need to feel your presence as I answer all of these questions with honesty. Then Lord, I need your help in making all the answers "yes" to these questions. Lord, I feel you as I confidently know you will meet me here today. I love you. Amen.

Ecclesiastes 2:26
*For to the person who pleases Him God gives wisdom and knowledge and joy; but to the sinner He gives the work of gathering and heaping up, that he may give to one who pleases God. This also is vanity and a striving after the wind and a feeding on it.*

I have never seen this before in all of my studies that God will allow the wicked to work hard gathering up wealth, success, material things, only to give to those who please God. So much of the world's philosophy is to acquire the most toys then hoard them for your own pleasure. But, God says, WHOA, these things are for the ones who please me. Hand them over.

This is a real wake up call for many. What you strive for in vanity can be like chasing the wind. So, why not begin giving today?

Dear God I feel your presence nudging me not to vainly pile up worldly possessions only to lose it. Lord, forgive me and help me to be a giver starting today. I love you. Amen.

Ecclesiastes 9:7

*Go your way, eat your bread with joy, and drink your wine with a cheerful heart [if you are righteous, wise, and in the hands of God], for God has already accepted your works.*

This is so encouraging to all of us. God is saying simply, enjoy your life, eat, maybe have a glass of wine if it doesn't cause you or someone else to stumble, and have a cheerful heart because He already has accepted you!

There is not one thing we can do to earn our way to heaven. Salvation is not a to-do list. Salvation comes from having a deep, personal relationship with the Living God and Son. Enjoy life and know you will see Jesus in heaven one day.

Dear God, thank you so much that I don't have to earn your love and acceptance. Thank you that you look at my heart and my love for you. I feel your presence today as my heart calls you Father. I love you. Amen.

Isaiah 29:19
*The meek also shall increase their joy in the Lord, and the poor among men shall rejoice and exult in the Holy One of Israel.*

Meek can be feeling peaceful and being humbly patient. Sometimes for me this is incredibly hard to do. I am a type A personality and to be meek seems weak. But, as I read this today, I am reminded that the meek shall inherit the earth.

Today ask yourself, am I peaceful? Do I wait patiently for things or for answers from God? I know I have to work on this personally because I really need an increase of Joy in my life. Where is the strength for life, it is the JOY in the Lord.

Dear God, please forgive me for being pushy and impatient so much of the time. Lord, forgive me for being anxious. Lord, I want to feel your presence today as peace runs through my soul and patience becomes easier for me. Thank you for reminding me the meek shall inherit the earth. I love you. Amen.

Isaiah 49:13
*Sing for joy, O heavens, and be joyful,*
*O earth, and break forth into singing, O*
*mountains! For the Lord has comforted His*
*people and will have compassion upon His*
*afflicted.*

We all need comforted in life. Only God
can really comfort on the level many of
us need. Only God can comfort a mother
who has lost a child to death. Only God
can comfort a woman whose husband
announced he wants a divorce. Only God
can comfort when cancer is diagnosed.

Remember today, that God is a God of
compassion. He never wants to see us in
agony or sorrow. God has always been the
helper to the afflicted. He is calling you
today to feel his comfort.

Dear God thank you for having such a
heart for the hurting. Lord thank you for
comforting broken hearts and painful
realities. Lord I feel your presence today as
I allow you to comfort like no other. I love
you. Amen.

<u>Matthew 5:3</u>
*Blessed (happy, to be envied, and spiritually prosperous - with life-joy and satisfaction in God's favor and salvation, regardless of their outward conditions) are the poor in spirit (the humble, who rate themselves insignificant), for theirs is the kingdom of heaven!*

Who ever thought that being poor in spirit and humble would be such a value that it might be envied? Only in God's Kingdom! God looks upon the poor in spirit as rich and the humble as significant.

Isn't this awesome? We all get so puffed up in the world's standards of success and significance and many of us don't add up to much. The enemy loves us to use this standard and inflate our pride and all. But, God loves the poor in spirit and humble because we are the ones who need him the most.

Dear God, I need you. I humbly bow at your feet today to feel you presence in making me feel significant no matter what the world calls me. I love you. Amen.

<u>Matthew 5:7</u>
*Blessed (happy, to be envied, and spiritually
prosperous-- with life-joy and satisfaction
in God's favor and salvation, regardless of
their outward conditions) are the merciful,
for they shall obtain mercy!*

We don't hear a lot about mercy. Today I
looked up the meaning; it is defined as kind,
lenient, forgiving, tender, and sympathetic.

God reminded me that by the measure
of mercy we give out to others, that is
the measure He will extend mercy to us.
So I ask myself how kind am I? Would
people use lenient, forgiving, tender, and
sympathetic as words to describe me? If not,
I need to really work on being more merciful
to all.

Dear God, please help me to extend mercy
to all I see. Lord, forgive me for being too
hard on people. Lord, I want you to extend
mercy on me that measures a lifetime
because I will never have it all together and
be faultless. Let me feel your mercy and
help me to extend more today. I love you.

Matthew 13:44
*The kingdom of heaven is like something precious buried in a field, which a man found and hid again; then in his joy he goes and sells all he has and buys that field.*

You know with all of the ministries that God has blessed me with, they all have the central focus that God turns our trash into treasures for the Kingdom. Right when the enemy thinks he has us full of shame, we hope God steps in through our ministry and says, nothing separates you from God's love.

Heaven is a buried treasure. Are you willing to sell all that you have to live there forever with God? The joy today and the presence of God can be when you accept that God is with you forever no matter how bad we fail.

Dear Father, thank you for turning my mistakes, my trash, into treasures and stories of victory that bring you glory. Thank you for loving me always. I feel your presence when I just think you love me just as I am. I love you. Amen.

<u>Luke 15:7</u>
*Thus, I tell you, there will be more joy
in heaven over one [especially] wicked
person who repents (changes his mind,
abhorring his errors and misdeeds, and
determines to enter upon a better course
of life) than over ninety-nine righteous
persons who have no need of repentance.*

Today make a commitment to yourself and
to God that you will diligently seek that one
person who is lost in sin and help them to
find God again. God needs all of us to do
this, and think how many lives would be
saved if we all just helped one come back to
him.

God encourages us to help others by saying
that if we help one person turn from their
sinful ways, then it covers a multitude of our
own sins. With God, everything is win-win
with him!

Dear God, show me who I need to help turn
from sin. Lord, I want to help you reach the
lost. Thank you, Lord, for turning my life
around. I love you. Amen.

<u>John 15:11</u>
*I have told you these things, that My joy
and delight may be in you, and that your joy
and gladness may be of full measure and
complete and overflowing.*

God wants us to have joy. It was never his
plan for us to be sad and down. God wants
us to have joy in our heart. The best way for
us to turn our sadness into Joy is to delight
in the fact that we dwell in this life with
God, and we will live eternally with him in
heaven.

Ask God to overflow you today with joy
and gladness. As you thank him that He will
save us from all pain and sorrow in the end,
let your heart be lightened and joyful in this
knowledge. Feel the presence of the Lord in
the fullness of knowing you will not live in
sorrow in heaven.

Dear God, please overflow my heart with joy
as I declare victory over death and sorrow.
Help me to refocus when I get down that you
alone will save me, and I will have happiness
forever with you. I love you. Amen

<u>John 16:24</u>
*Up to this time you have not asked a [single] thing in My Name [as presenting all that I AM]; but now ask and keep on asking and you will receive, so that your joy (gladness, delight) may be full and complete.*

This is a great verse for all of us to say everyday. Ask away to God for what you need, but always do it in his name. What is God to you today? What do you need him to be for you today?

I need God to be my defender today. So, I say Lord, I need your help in keeping me from getting my feelings hurt today from criticism. Lord, please be my defender. In your name Father, I ask and I believe I will receive your protection.

Dear God, I need you to be _____ for me today. Lord, let me feel your presence in the way you answer my needs. Lord, I know if I ask it in your name you will answer. I love you. Amen.

*Day 286*

<u>John 17:13</u>
*And now I am coming to You; I say these things while I am still in the world, so that My joy may be made full and complete and perfect in them [that they may experience My delight fulfilled in them, that My enjoyment may be perfected in their own souls, that they may have My gladness within them, filling their hearts].*

Jesus was hoping that the people who actually saw and touched him would make their lives complete with joy. For us the joy comes from the example He left for us to follow and the words He left to guide us.

Jesus experienced Joy when He saw others follow him and perfect their souls through him. Follow Jesus today and allow him to fill your hearts with gladness and joy.

Dear Father, thank you for your only Son who left us with a great example and words to guide us through the maze of life. Lord, I claim your Son as my Savior and feel your presence with joy that overflows my heart. I love you. Amen.

<u>Acts 2:28</u>

*You have made known to me the ways of life; You will enrapture me [diffusing my soul with joy] with and in Your presence.*

Again, we see that God already knows the way our life will go. As long as we stay in obedience to what He has called for us to do, He will direct our every move.

Enrapture means to delight beyond measure. God is waiting to do that for all of us. It's not just what I think; it is what the scripture tells us. God will give us the delight that is beyond measure and joy. Find it today.

Dear God, I long to be enraptured in your love and joy. Let me feel your presence as my soul wraps around the thoughts of you loving and directing my life and showering me with your joy. I love you. Amen.

<u>Romans 5:3</u>
*Moreover [let us also be full of joy now!] let us exult and triumph in our troubles and rejoice in our sufferings, knowing that pressure and affliction and hardship produce patient and unswerving endurance.*

Amen to that. Hardships and trials do produce one positive thing - endurance. As Christ followers, we must have endurance. Paul states this life is not a sprint but a marathon. It takes a lot of stamina to run a marathon.

In your troubles, sufferings, and afflictions try to stay focused on what God is trying to work out in us. God uses these trials to burn more of us off and fill us up with him. Ask him, "God what do you need to show me that you are producing in this trial?"

Dear God, I know not one tear goes unnoticed. I know you don't let us suffer for nothing. Lord. Let me feel your presence as I look for what I need to lose that will showcase more of you. I love you. Amen.

<u>Romans 5:4</u>
*And endurance (fortitude) develops
maturity of character (approved faith and
tried integrity). And character [of this sort]
produces [the habit of] joyful and confident
hope of eternal salvation.*

We all need more of this in our daily
lives. Endurance, fortitude, approved faith,
integrity, character, the habit of joy, and
confident hope. I can't say I have ever seen
a list that seems so hard to accomplish.

The Lord is calling us to work on every area
listed above starting right now. Every one
of these traits is obtainable only through the
power of Christ. Today, we all must fall to
our knees and cry out to God to give us the
power to develop these traits.

Dear God, as I read the list above it seems
almost near to impossible to possess these
traits. God, I know you are the God that
makes the impossible, possible, and Lord, I
want to feel your presence as you develop
these Godly characteristics in me daily
starting today. I love you. Amen.

Romans 15:13
*May the God of your hope so fill you with all joy and peace in believing [through the experience of your faith] that by the power of the Holy Spirit you may abound and be overflowing (bubbling over) with hope.*

That's what I want, the bubbling over of hope that only comes from God. Lord, my hope is that you will fill us all with peace and joy. My faith that you are indeed the power that lives in me through the Holy Spirit is all that keeps me going many days.

The Lord needs more of us as living testimonies of the overflowing hope that lives within us. The world today is so dark and hopeless that God is counting on us to have the joy that bubbles over for the world to see.

Dear God, let me feel your presence today as you fill me with hope that bubbles over. Hope that one day no more pain, sorrow, or trials will be experienced. Hope that you will come and take us to live in your love forever in Heaven. I love you. Amen.

<u>1 Corinthians 13:13</u>

*And so faith, hope, love abide [faith - conviction and belief respecting man's relation to God and divine things; hope - joyful and confident expectation of eternal salvation; love - true affection for God and man, growing out of God's love for and in us], these three; but the greatest of these is love.*

The greatest of faith, hope, and love is Love. What good are faith and hope if we do not love? What good is it to perform all kinds of good works but not love your neighbor?

The biggest testimony is the one at home. If your kids, husband, friends, and family can't back what you speak, then, your words are for nothing. Your love and testimony begins at home.

Dear God, let my life be true on every level and in every circumstance. Help me to love greater and to show it more. Lord, forgive me and help me to be true to my testimony at home and everywhere. I love you. Amen.

Galatians 5:22
*But the fruit of the [Holy] Spirit [the work which His presence within accomplishes] is love, joy (gladness), peace, patience (an even temper, forbearance), kindness, goodness (benevolence), faithfulness,*

The only way to achieve love, peace, patience, an even temper, kindness, goodness, and faithfulness is through the power of the Holy Spirit. How do you get the Holy Spirit? You confess that Jesus is the Son of the living God who died for your sins on the cross, then go and be baptized. Then the Holy Spirit will come into you and strengthen who you are.

Dear God, today as a believer I ask the Holy Spirit to get stirred up like never before. I ask that I feel your presence today as the fruits of the Spirit are elevated in my Spirit. Lord, today if I am not a believer, I ask Jesus to come into my heart as I make him my Lord and Savior so that the Holy Spirit can live in me and be my helper. I love you. Amen.

<u>Galatians 6:4</u>
*But let every person carefully scrutinize
and examine and test his own conduct
and his own work. He can then have the
personal satisfaction and joy of doing
something commendable [in itself alone]
without [resorting to] boastful comparison
with his neighbor.*

You know I used to love to say that as
soon as I could afford to buy a new car,
I was sure someone close to me would
buy a nicer and more expensive one too.
Somebody will always be able to one-up us
in the world.

In our spiritual walk, we must not dare to
compare to what others are doing for the
Kingdom. We each have our own unique
purpose. Follow your own purpose because
God does NOT compare us to anyone.

Dear God, help me to feel your presence
today as I gather personal satisfaction in
knowing I did what you have asked me to
do. Even if my task looks small to others, I
have the joy of knowing I completed your
wish. I love you. Amen.

Hebrews 3:6
*But Christ (the Messiah) was faithful over
His [own Father's] house as a Son [and
Master of it]. And it is we who are [now
members] of this house, if we hold fast
and firm to the end our joyful and exultant
confidence and sense of triumph in our
hope [in Christ].*

We are God's house, the temple of God. We
must be faithful to God with everything we
are and everything we do. We must hold fast
and firm to what we know is true and good.

God has provided triumph in the hope that if
we stand firm and faithful there will be joy
for a lifetime. Don't let the enemy in your
house. Keep the eye gate, mouth gate, and
ear gate at attention always. We are the gate
keepers and faithful owners of our house,
and God will reward our firm stance.

Dear God, thank you for helping me keep
watch over my house which is your temple
Lord, help me keep the enemy out. Lord,
let me feel your presence as you help guard
what I see, hear, and say. I love you. Amen.

<u>Hebrews 12:11</u>

*For the time being no discipline brings joy, but seems grievous and painful; but afterwards it yields a peaceable fruit of righteousness to those who have been trained by it [a harvest of fruit which consists in righteousness - in conformity to God's will in purpose, thought, and action, resulting in right living and right standing with God].*

Whoever said being disciplined was fun? In the past, I resented the struggles and trials so much I would get angry with God. As the trials turned into victory, I started seeing the harvest of these tough times and discipline.

God only chastens the ones He loves. Victory after victory has shown me God was working to let good come from bad. All the pain was to make me more like God.

Dear God, thank you for the pain that makes me a better Christ follower. Let me feel your presence today as the glory of you shines through the victory of my trials. I love you. Amen.

James 1:2
*Consider it wholly joyful, my brethren,*
*whenever you are enveloped in or*
*encounter trials of any sort or fall into*
*various temptations.*

Not only does God say when we encounter
"trials" but when we fall into various
"temptations." This tells me God knows we
will all surely fail him. He knows that we
are weak. He knows that we will all fall into
temptation and sin.

I never really count it as joy when I get
enveloped in sin and trials. Here God knows
that not one sin or failed attempt at living
Holy will be wasted. As I have stated before,
God has used my sin and shame, my trash,
and turned it into his treasure. The enemy is
going to wish he had never touched me!

Dear God, I thank you for this today. I know
I will fail you, but I also know you love me.
Lord, thank you for not letting one failure
cost me my life forever with you. Let me
feel your presence as I thank you for not
wasting one of my hurts. I love you. Amen.

1 Peter 4:14

*If you are censured and suffer abuse
[because you bear] the name of Christ,
blessed [are you - happy, fortunate, to be
envied, with life-joy, and satisfaction in
God's favor and salvation, regardless of
your outward condition], because the Spirit
of glory, the Spirit of God, is resting upon
you. On their part He is blasphemed, but
on your part He is glorified.*

We will all be tried by the world, and some
of us even persecuted. The world hates us
when we stand up for what is right and true.
It can be in your neighborhood, at work,
with other parents, or even at your church.

Dear God, I really need you today. It seems
I fight the enemy all the time. My neighbors
don't understand why we don't participate
in gambling, other parents don't understand
our strict curfew, the church doesn't understand why we love sinners and offer mercy
and grace to a fallen pastor. Please let me
feel your presence today as you heal my
hurts and wounds. I love you. Amen.

<u>3 John 1:4</u>
*I have no greater joy than this, to hear that my [spiritual] children are living their lives in the Truth.*

I love this scripture as a Mother. I am living this out today. It gives me no greater joy than to know that my children know the Lord and have claimed Jesus as their personal Savior. However, this doesn't mean they don't disappoint me or make terrible choices.

I try to keep my mind on their eternal lives. As I write this, I have children that are 15, 16, and 19. They are in the midst of enemy lines constantly. So, I take comfort in this scripture and rejoice knowing that they do know the way the truth and light, Jesus.

Dear God, I know you delight in knowing we and our children are living in the truth. Lord, help me to feel your presence as I give my children to you at the altar like Abraham and Isaac, for my children were yours first. I love you. Amen.

<u>Revelation 19:7</u>
*Let us rejoice and shout for joy [exulting
and triumphant]! Let us celebrate and
ascribe to Him glory and honor, for the
marriage of the Lamb [at last] has come,
and His bride has prepared herself.*

The thing I anticipate the most about
meeting God, is the terrific and magnificent
celebration that will be going on! I always
go back to the prodigal son when I think
of God throwing a party. The son's father
went to all lengths and expense to welcome
his lost son home.

That's what God is preparing for us. A
huge party and celebration called,
"Welcome Home." My heart sings for joy
that one day I truly will be welcomed home
into heaven, and I will leave this dark
world of pain.

Dear God, thank you for this today. My
heart hopes for that special day at the
Homecoming Celebration. I feel the joy
and hope in my heart as I feel your love
in the preparation of that day. I love you.
Amen.

<u>Psalm 107:20</u>
*He sends forth His word and heals*
*them and rescues them from the pit and*
*destruction.*

Have you ever felt you as if you were in
a pit of destruction? I have been there,
and it was the worst experience in my
life. It takes me back to Psalms 40 where
David says, "He pulled me out of the
horrible pit." I am a living testimony to this
scripture of being pulled out of a pit.

My marriage was dead, I was in enormous
personal debt, my children were sick, and
so many dark places were in my life. BUT
GOD, He reached from the heavens, pulled
me out of the pit, and delivered me!

Dear God, please help me get out of this
situation today. Lord, let me feel your
presence as I feel a new sense of victory
of darkness and sin, Lord, thank you for
rescuing all of us. I love you. Amen.

Psalm 136:24
*And rescued us from our enemies, for His
mercy and loving-kindness endure forever;*

Today I needed this more than ever. The
enemy knows my biggest weakness is to
be liked by all. The ministry is growing at
such a miraculous pace. I am amazed at
God. While I am experiencing supernatural
growth and experiences with God that are
indescribable, I am being mocked, judged,
and ridiculed. My heart is broken as the
enemy hits me at my weakest link.

So, today, join me as we pray for our
enemies. Let's lift up those in prayer that
the enemy is using to hurt us or have hurt
us. Then, let's release these hurts and
people and allow God to heal our wounds.
Let's feel his presence today as we rest in
his love and peace.

Dear God, heal my heart and my hurts. Let
me feel your peace today as I release the
pain of today and yesterday. I rest in your
loving arms. I love you. Amen.

Proverbs 20:22
*Do not say, I will repay evil; wait
[expectantly] for the Lord, and He will
rescue you.*

This seems impossible for me some days. I
want to retaliate. I want to state back the truth
to the lies. I want to kick and scream at the
insanity of the accusations or untruths. BUT
God says right here, do not pay evil with evil.

Today, I ask the Lord to help me be quieter. I
ask him to help me not to get so dramatic and
oversensitive to offenses. I ask the Lord
to help me control my tongue and my temper
so that the enemy does not help me to ruin
my witness!

Dear God, please forgive me for the times I
just lose it. Forgive me when my voice gets
louder, and my frustrations ooze out of every
pore of my body. Please help those who I
have been angry at find forgiveness for me
in their hearts. Lord, help me to feel your
presence today as I control my tongue and
temper. I love you Lord, and thank you for
rescuing me from myself. Amen.

<u>Lamentations 3:58</u>
*O Lord, You have pleaded the causes of my soul [You have managed my affairs and You have protected my person and my rights]; You have rescued and redeemed my life!*

I believe this with all my heart, that Jesus pleads our case before our Heavenly Father. Jesus has been here. Jesus has been ridiculed, betrayed, and heartbroken. Jesus has felt the pain as a human and the temptations of the enemy!

I know that Jesus pleads our cases daily through his blood He shed on the cross for each one of us. I know He says, "Father, Laine didn't mean it. Her heart is just broken."

Dear God, thank you that Jesus does know the fears, pain, and temptation that trips us all up. Lord, thank you for the blood of Christ that washes us clean before you even we fail. Lord, forgive us and thank you that you allow Jesus to plead our case. I love you. Amen.

Ezekiel 34:12

*As a shepherd seeks out his sheep in the day that he is among his flock that are scattered, so will I seek out My sheep; and I will rescue them out of all places where they have been scattered in the day of clouds and thick darkness.*

What an awesome word today that Jesus as our shepherd seeks us out even when we are scattered or in darkness. That means no matter how far off track we get or how deep in the darkness of sin, Jesus will seek us out. Amazing his love is that vast for all of us!

Jesus is waiting for all of us to call his name and surrender our needs and hearts. Ask yourself today, "Do I need Jesus?" Then know He is right there waiting and searching for you.

Dear God, thank you for the love of Jesus. Let me feel you today as I feel the spirit of being found. Lord, forgive me, and I need you. I love you. Amen.

<u>Mark 13:20</u>
*And unless the Lord had shortened the days, no human being would be saved (rescued); but for the sake of the elect, His chosen ones (those whom He picked out for Himself), He has shortened the days.*

WHOA! It says right here God knew how hard and how cruel it was to make us live too long down here on earth! God reused all mankind by cutting down the number of days we would live on earth.

God has picked each one of us out himself as it says in this scripture today. Do you call yourself the child of God? Do you know that you are the son or daughter of the most High King? Do you know that God knows you by name?

Dear God, today I long to feel your presence as a daughter or a son. I want to feel your love for me as a Father who loves his child. I thank you that you know me by name and that you have chosen me to be yours. I love you. Amen.

<u>Luke 11:4</u>
*And forgive us our sins, for we ourselves
also forgive everyone who is indebted to us
[who has offended us or done us wrong].
And bring us not into temptation but rescue
us from evil.*

Here it is. We must forgive others as God
forgives us. But also, we must forgive ourselves. Why is it that many times it is easier
to forgive others, yet we are the last ones to
forgive ourselves?

Is there a sin or shame for which you have
not forgiven yourself? Is there a sin that
you have not confessed and need
forgiveness? If so, don't delay. Ask God
for forgiveness of all of your sins, confess
them, and then moving on by receiving the
forgiveness.

Dear Father, please forgive me. Please
forgive these specific sins I confess today.
Lord, I am sorry. Help me to do better. Help
me Lord, to feel your presence as I receive
this gift of forgiveness and the feeling of no
condemnation. I love you. Amen

<u>2 Corinthians 1:10</u>
*[For it is He] Who rescued and saved us*
*from such a perilous death, and He will*
*still rescue and save us; in and on Him we*
*have set our hope (our joyful and confident*
*expectation) that He will again deliver us*
*[from danger and destruction and draw us*
*to Himself],*

Not only will God rescue us, save us,
deliver us, but He draws himself closer to
us. God will bring us out of danger and
destruction so that we may see him in the
rescue. Today, I ask you to reflect and
remember some times in your life you were
in danger. Can you to see where God was in
all of that?

Do you see God rescuing you, his hand in
it all? Do you see how God saved you from
eternal death? God will continue to draw us
out of danger to see him in our rescue.

Dear God, thank you for never giving up on
me. Thank you for rescuing me all the time
so that I don't live in death forever. I love
you. Amen.

<u>Galatians 1:4</u>
*Who gave (yielded) Himself up [to atone]
for our sins [and to save and sanctify us],
in order to rescue and deliver us from this
present wicked age and world order, in
accordance with the will and purpose and
plan of our God and Father—*

Oh, how I relate to this scripture. When I
start throwing a pity party of how hard this
walk of following Christ is, I immediately
go to this scripture and see that Jesus was
obedient to death! In order to save all of us,
Jesus knew He would be crucified, and still
walked down the road that would lead him
to it. Would you?

What have you sacrificed for Jesus lately?
What have you had to yield to the Holy
Spirit in order to grow more like Jesus?
Don't throw a pity party but a celebration
that Jesus was obedient to death so we may
live eternal.

Dear God, please forgive my pity party.
I know Jesus, touch me today to give me
strength to follow you. I love you. Amen.

<u>1 Thessalonians 1:10</u>
*And [how you] look forward to and await*
*the coming of His Son from heaven, Whom*
*He raised from the dead - Jesus, Who*
*personally rescues and delivers us out of*
*and from the wrath [bringing punishment]*
*which is coming [upon the impenitent] and*
*draws us to Himself [investing us with all*
*the privileges and rewards of the new life in*
*Christ, the Messiah].*

Amen! I am waiting for that day! Oh to
look in the heavens and see Jesus coming
to get me from all of this darkness and pain.
No more tears, no more sorrow, no more
broken hearts, no more sickness! This is
what keeps me going everyday to know that
Jesus is really coming back!

Are you ready right now for Jesus to return?
Are you surrendered and saved? Jesus will
reward you today and in the eternal life
when you personally ask him to rescue you
and deliver you!

Dear God, thank you for saving me. Thank
you for Jesus and the life eternal with you, I
look forward to that day! I love you. *Page 315*

<u>2 Peter 2:9</u>
*Now if [all these things are true, then be sure] the Lord knows how to rescue the godly out of temptations and trials, and how to keep the ungodly under chastisement until the day of judgment and doom,*

Don't let the enemy lie to you anymore today that God does not have a plan for you. God always knows what is going on. Here today we see that God has a plan to even get us out of temptations and trials. I like to look at it like a fire drill and God knows how to show us out of dangers and the burn of sin.

So tell the enemy he is a liar if you are in the midst of infidelity and you feel there is no way out. Or if you are in personal debt that looks like it can never be fixed. God has a plan for escape. Ask God today to reveal your plan of rescue.

Dear God, let me feel you presence as you answer my cries for help. Lord, touch my ears so that I can hear your plans of escape for me. I love you. Amen.

<u>Jonah 4:6</u>
*And the Lord God prepared a gourd and made it to come up over Jonah, that it might be a shade over his head, to deliver him from his evil situation. So Jonah was exceedingly glad [to have the protection] of the gourd.*

Oh Lord, I know you have prepared many gourds for me. Let me, Lord, never forget all of the times you have given me a way out. Lord, thank you for healing my marriage. Lord, thank you for making my sick children well. Lord, you have provided so many ways to deliver me from evil.

Today, Lord we ask you to deliver us from evil. Lord, we ask that we feel your presence in the knowledge you are our protection. Lord, let my heart be filled with gladness today as I rejoice in the hope that you are my protection. Lord, please deliver me from evil so that I may live forever with you in heaven. I love you. Amen.

Deuteronomy 33:27
*The eternal God is your refuge and dwelling place, and underneath are the everlasting arms; He drove the enemy before you and thrust them out, saying, Destroy!*

Last night as I was fighting fear for my teenagers and the ministry, I visualized myself lying under the arms of God. I allowed myself to see my face lying on his chest with my shoulders tucked safely under his arms. I claimed him as my dwelling place.

Today if you are anxious or fear is consuming you, I challenge you to close your eyes and visualize yourself tucking your head under God's arm and resting on his chest. Ask him to give you rest and peace. God is our dwelling place, and his arms are everlasting.

Dear God, I feel your presence as I close my eyes and see myself resting on you. Lord, I feel your arms wrap themselves around me to keep me safe from fear and evil. You are my refuge. I love you. Amen.

<u>2 Samuel 22:3</u>
*My God, my Rock, in Him will I take refuge; my Shield and the Horn of my salvation; my Stronghold and my Refuge, my Savior - You save me from violence.*

The next time you feel panicked or under attack, state these three facts: God you are my rock, God you are my refuge, and God you are my shield. Claim it out loud and as many times as you need to. Scream it if you need to.

When we claim decrees from God they are digested in our souls. Then, they manifest themselves into truths because we begin to believe them more and more as we speak them repeatedly. Today, speak these aloud many times, and if you are in a desperate way, or if you get in a tight spot, the truth will deliver you.

Thank you Lord, that you are my rock, my refuge, and my shield. Lord, I surrender my life to you. I will speak these truths about you until I know that you are my refuge. I love you. Amen.

## 2 Samuel 22:31

*As for God, His way is perfect; the word of the Lord is tried. He is a Shield to all those who trust and take refuge in Him.*

Isn't it great to know that there is a "perfect?" God is perfect. His ways are perfect. His words are perfect. His timing is perfect. His plans are perfect. When you realize this, you will be able to trust him in every area of your life. This will give you the confidence to know He is the only place of retreat and refuge from this world we live in.

Do you truly acknowledge that God's ways, words, timing, and plans are perfect? Do you yield to him your ways, plans, and words? Ask God today to make his plans, word, and ways yours.

Dear God, I thank you that you are perfect. Help me to grow my trust in you, Lord. Let me run to you alone in times of trouble. Lord, help me to yield my plans, desires, and words to what you want for me. I know your will is best and perfect. I love you. Amen.

<u>Psalm 7:1</u>
*O LORD my God, in You I take refuge and put my trust; save me from all those who pursue and persecute me, and deliver me,*

God knows we will be pursued by evil. He also knows we will be persecuted by the world. That is why it is so important to feel his presence daily, so that we take refuge in his ways. God is the only way to be delivered from the evil of the world.

What are we turning to for deliverance? Do we drink to relax, do we gamble to escape, do we take drugs to sleep and make us feel better? Be honest today and acknowledge what it is we turn to for deliverance. If it is not God, then turn to him today to deliver you from the world's evil and pain.

Dear God, I need you today more than ever. I must feel your presence through delivering me from evil and the things I do to escape the world and pain. God, I ask you to deliver me and replace it all with you. The Lord is my deliverer and refuge. I love you. Amen.

<u>Psalm 9:9</u>
*The Lord also will be a refuge and a high tower for the oppressed, a refuge and a stronghold in times of trouble (high cost, destitution, and desperation).*

Are you desperate or destitute today? Do you need God on such a level it is desperate? God needs you to know today that He is your refuge and your high tower. He is a God to hold on to in times of desperation.

God showed me recently that He is my high tower. He revealed to me that He doesn't just see for miles and miles past where I am today but in days. God has already ordained our days. God knows literally, what will come tomorrow for us. If you are oppressed, destitute, or desperate, you must know that God knows exactly where you are and exactly where your days are headed.

Oh Father, thank you for being my high tower. Lord, thank you for knowing right where I am today and where I will be tomorrow. I feel your presence today as I rest in your refuge. I love you. Amen.

Psalm 14:6
*You [evildoers] would put to shame and*
*confound the plans of the poor and patient,*
*but the Lord is his safe refuge.*

I do believe there are people that the
enemy uses just to do his evil plans. I am
convinced many people in the world do
things that are motivated by the enemy in
them. But God always has a plan to divert
the plans of the enemy.

Today, ask God to reveal the people who
may be planning evil against you. Make
sure you go to God about all of our
relationships. The enemy is cunning and sly
and sometimes appears to be very meek.
Then you will be deceived until there
destructive plan is realized in our lives.

Dear God, thank you that you provide
safety. Lord, please in the name of Jesus
bind all enemy influences in my life and
my loved ones lives. In the blood of Christ,
deliver us from evil so that your perfect
plans can be lived out in my life. I love you.
Amen.

<u>Psalm 18:2</u>
*The Lord is my Rock, my Fortress, and
my Deliverer; my God, my keen and firm
Strength in Whom I will trust and take
refuge, my Shield, and the Horn of my
salvation, my High Tower.*

We must all depend on God's strength
daily! We can not do this life on earth with
out him. Allow God to be your fortress.
Fortress can be described as exceptional
security.

I need security. I need physical security
from harm. I need security from bad people
who plan to hurt me emotionally. Also,
I need security that will protect my soul
from the enemy. Do you need a new level
of security in your life? Ask God to be your
security system and to sound the alarm
when danger is present.

Dear God, today allow me to feel your
presence by securing me emotionally,
physically, and spiritually. Lord, I run to
you and ask that you sound the security
alarm if I am in danger. I love you. Amen.

Psalm 18:30

*As for God, His way is perfect! The word of the Lord is tested and tried; He is a shield to all those who take refuge and put their trust in Him.*

God has been tested since the beginning of time. He has passed these tests every time. The enemy has the religious spirit covering so many believers with the stronghold that God is not faithful and He is not good. But God's ways are perfect and proven.

Don't be deceived anymore trying to justify the wrongs we do. The enemy is a liar. God is with us in times of despair and celebration. He is faithful, and He is good. Break free from the religious spirit of abandonment.

Dear God, deliver me from the religious spirit that lies to me constantly. Lord, bind it in the name of Jesus, so I can be delivered to a new way of thinking. Lord, you are perfect, and you are proven true. I love you. Amen.

<u>Psalm 27:1</u>
*[[A Psalm] of David. ] THE LORD is my Light and my Salvation - whom shall I fear or dread? The Lord is the Refuge and Stronghold of my life - of whom shall I be afraid?*

If God is your salvation, what should we fear? What is there to dread? Even if you are in a down season of your life, just know God is never late. He is always waiting on us; we are not waiting on him. He is a God of love, and He is not to blame.

All we have to do is acknowledge him, and He will run to the rescue. God will never let his children stay in a season of sadness longer than we can take. He is there always!

Dear God, please let me feel you presence today as I cry out to you. Lord, I acknowledge that you are my Refuge, and I know that have no need for fear anymore. I love you. Amen.

<u>Psalm 31:2</u>
*Bow down Your ear to me, deliver me speedily! Be my Rock of refuge, a strong Fortress to save me!*

God does hear us when we call to him. He does not wait a minute too late to come to us. Sometimes we must exercise patience waiting on him to do what we need. In the meantime, - I like to say it is a MEAN TIME - we must dig deep and ask God what we are to learn during the wait.

As I look back at long periods of waiting, I see God's hands refining and fine tuning me. During the times of waiting, I had to rely on him in a whole new way. I had to dig deeper and find hope and courage. God is waiting for us to do that today.

Dear God, please help me to dig deeper to figure out what I need to change. Lord, let me feel you as I listen for you to speak and reveal the things I need to change so I can be more like you. I love you. Amen.

<u>Psalm 37:39</u>
*But the salvation of the [consistently] righteous is of the Lord; He is their Refuge and secure Stronghold in the time of trouble.*

The key word here is consistent. Are we constantly adhering to the same principles of God on a daily basis? Do we show the world through our actions, not words, that the Lord is our top priority. Do people see the fruits of the spirit, attributes of God's character, being lived out in my life?

The challenge is not to live some days good and for the Lord, and then other days live as we want. We must consistently strive to be more like Jesus daily. Ask yourself today, am I living consistently for the Lord?

Dear God, don't let me deceive myself. Help me to answer to myself if I live more for you than I do for myself. Lord, forgive me. Help me to be more like you everyday and to live more consistently as a Christ follower. Lord, I want the world to see more of you in me. I love you. Amen.

Psalm 37:40
*And the Lord helps them and delivers*
*them; He delivers them from the wicked*
*and saves them, because they trust and*
*take refuge in Him.*

TRUST and OBEY for there is no other
way has been said for years and years. We
must trust the Lord even when it does not
make sense. This is the most difficult area
I work on in my personal life - knowing
that when things do not look good in the
natural, God has me covered.

God says that He is the refuge for those
who trust him. Trusting God in the darkest
hour can be a difficult task. But I love to
say that I would rather error on the side of
God, that He indeed is going to save me,
than to error on the side of man where it
truly is impossible.

Dear God, help me to trust you more in the
darkest hour. Lord, help me to see you in
glimpses of hope. Lord, let me feel your
presence as you touch me in the neediest
times. I love you. Amen.

Psalm 40:4
*Blessed (happy, fortunate, to be envied)
is the man who makes the Lord his refuge
and trust, and turns not to the proud or to
followers of false gods.*

I want to be blessed! I want to be happy
and fortunate. It says right here that if we
trust in God this will follow. I know this
to be true. Even if the times are tough,
God always pulls us out of pits. When you
truly believe that in your heart, then the
enemy can't still the joy you find in God's
strength.

Happiness and fortune will never come to
those who are proud. Nor will it ever come
to the ones who make everything more of
a priority than God. That's why so many
people are miserable today.

Dear God, help me to make you my top
priority in my life. Lord, I want to be
happy and blessed, and I know it comes
only through you. Lord, let me feel you
today as I trust and know who you are. I
love you. Amen.

Psalm 46:1

*[To the Chief Musician. [A Psalm] of the sons of Korah, set to treble voices. A song.] GOD IS our Refuge and Strength [mighty and impenetrable to temptation], a very present and well-proved help in trouble.*

This verse is in my heart and ready to be spoken at a drop of a hat. Today memorize this verse. God, you are a very present help in any time of trouble. God truly is there even when you can't see him right away.

God is mighty. We don't talk about this enough. God has his hands on you and your future. He is a mighty God that will not let anything get in the way of his plans for you. He is mighty and a very present help in times of danger.

Dear God, thank you that you are mighty. Lord, let me feel you as I rest in the fact you know the plans for my life. Lord, I know that no demon in hell can keep your plans for my life from being a reality. I love you. Amen.

Psalm 57:1

*[To the Chief Musician; [set to the tune of]
"Do Not Destroy." A record of memorable
thoughts of David when he fled from Saul
in the cave.] BE MERCIFUL and gracious
to me, O God, be merciful and gracious
to me, for my soul takes refuge and finds
shelter and confidence in You; yes, in the
shadow of Your wings will I take refuge and
be confident until calamities and destructive
storms are passed.*

Calamities and storms are certain. God is
the refuge in the storm. God is merciful and
gracious. So many of the dark pits we get
into, we get there ourselves through trails of
sin.

Trust in God. Take refuge in the shadow of
his wing. Be confident that God will help
you out of the storms of life and that He will
make all things bad turn into good for his
glory.

Dear God, allow me to feel your safety today
as I rest in the shadow of your wing. Thank
you for your mercy and Love. I love you.

Psalm 59:16

*But I will sing of Your mighty strength and power; yes, I will sing aloud of Your mercy and loving-kindness in the morning; for You have been to me a defense (a fortress and a high tower) and a refuge in the day of my distress.*

Sometimes in the midst of troubles and darkness, it takes until morning to make sense of things. Also, the enemy loves to tell us that God doesn't have a clue of what we are encountering. But God is our defense.

God will show up. God is our high tower. God is our refuge in the days of distress. You must lay these scriptures of protection deep within your soul. The day is coming, if not today, that the enemy will try to keep you in sin, hopeless that God is not there.

Dear God, help me to write this on my heart. Help me to know that you are my high tower and refuge in times of trouble. Let me feel your love in my heart today. I love you. Amen.

<u>Psalm 62:8</u>
*Trust in, lean on, rely on, and have confidence in Him at all times, you people; pour out your hearts before Him. God is a refuge for us (a fortress and a high tower). Selah [pause, and calmly think of that]!*

Whom do you rely on? How many times have you been let down? How many times have you been betrayed? All of us would have to answer at least once to those questions. But if you ask yourself how many times God has let you down, the answer would surely be never.

I ask whom do we rely on, God or man? Who will be there for us twenty-four hours a day? Who is there in the darkest hour? Who is there to rescue us? Who is there to give us eternal life forever?

Dear God, please forgive me for relying on man too much. Lord, let me feel you today, as I know in my core that you are the only one I can count on always. I love you. Amen.

Psalm 71:1

*IN YOU, O Lord, do I put my trust and
confidently take refuge; let me never be put
to shame or confusion!*

We must pray often to God for the inner
knowledge that no shame or sin separates
us from the love of Christ. The enemy loves
to keep all of us under self-condemnation.
The enemy is best when he constantly
reminds us of all of our wrong doings and
sin.

Go before God today with confidence
knowing He loves you right where you
are! God knows we are never going to live
without sin. Don't let the enemy lie to you
today. You are God's child; all you have
to do is ask for forgiveness. God not only
forgives but forgets.

Dear God, please forgive me of my sin. I
am so sorry. Lord, I am so tired of beating
myself up for my failures. Lord, let me feel
you today as I accept your forgiveness and
the knowledge that you forget too. Bind
the enemy in the name of Jesus so I forgive
myself. I love you. Amen.

Psalm 91:4

*[Then] He will cover you with His pinions, and under His wings shall you trust and find refuge; His truth and His faithfulness are a shield and a buckler.*

Pinions are gears that interact and the larger gear (God) helps the smaller gear (us) to perform at its best. God will cover you as a larger gear that will enable you to do what He designed for you to do. His wings shall cover you in the dark times and when you are in pain.

Remember today that God is faithful. God will never leave you or forsake you. He is the truth of life. He is your refuge. Today feel his presence as you close your eyes and allow him to cover you. Allow God to put you under his wing and feel the safety and comfort in your heart.

Dear God, thank you for orchestrating my life. Thank you that you are with me always no matter where I am in my life. Lord, you are faithful and true. I love you. Amen.

<u>Psalm 118:8</u>
*It is better to trust and take refuge in the Lord than to put confidence in man.*

The world tells us to put our confidence in everything but God. Put your savings in a bank for retirement. Buy a big house and buy all the toys you can so that you look successful, and the world will treat you well. Everywhere you turn, we are tempted to put our confidence in what the world is selling us.

The big question today is, "Do you trust man more than God?" Really, in a panic do you call a friend before you call God? In times of despair, do you turn to a bottle or to God? When a child is astray do we turn everywhere instead of God? Trust in God, not man.

Dear God, help me to feel your presence today as I reach for you like never before. I cry to you. I ask for your hand in showing me where to go. Teach me, Lord, to come to you first in all ways. I love you. Amen.

<u>Proverbs 30:5</u>
*Every word of God is tried and purified;*
*He is a shield to those who trust and take*
*refuge in Him*

I looked up purified to better understand
the meaning of this scripture. Purified
means to free from guilt or evil. Therefore,
the word of God can free us from guilt and
from evil.

We must be believers who stay in the word.
We must daily get our spiritual feeding in
order to grow in him. His word is the key
to all of our lives down here. Without the
tried and purified word we are lost and
spiritually starving. The word of God is the
only place that gives life to us.

Dear God, thank you for your word. Lord,
reveal to me, as I am in your presence, the
word that applies directly to me. Lord, let
my ears hear what you need to speak to
me. Lord, help me daily to feed on the life
of the living word. I love you. Amen.

<u>Nahum 1:7</u>
*The Lord is good, a Strength and Stronghold in the day of trouble; He knows (recognizes, has knowledge of, and understands) those who take refuge and trust in Him.*

The Lord is good. Sometimes this one scripture is what gets me through the tough times. When things in my life are all falling apart, I have found out if I speak that over my life, God comes quicker to the rescue.

God is good all the time. There are many times we have to diligently seek him in the darkness. When we are in trials, it seems impossible that God could know what is going on. Today, speak this over your life that God is good. Then every time you are in a tight spot in life remember that God is good. This may be the only nugget that gets you through it.

Dear God, help me to know that you are good. No matter what it looks like in the natural, you are here, and you are good. Lord, let me feel your presence today as my hope is reactivated in you. I love you. Amen.

Deuteronomy 12:10
*But when you go over the Jordan and
dwell in the land which the Lord your God
causes you to inherit, and He gives you rest
from all your enemies round about so that
you dwell in safety,*

The Jordan was the trial they had to get
over to get to the promise of God. Today I
ask you, "What is your Jordan?" What is it
that you are facing that if you could only get
through it then you should get to what God
has planned for you?

Many trials we must endure to get to where
we need to go. I have found that many of
my painful times were the exact things that
had to happen to make me who I am in
Christ today. What is it that you must get
THROUGH to get TO your destiny today?

Dear God, help me to learn all I can as I
go through this trial so I can get to where I
need to go. Lord, let me feel you today as I
surrender in this day to get to where I need
to go for you. I love you. Amen.

<u>Deuteronomy 20:4</u>
*For the Lord your God is He Who goes with you to fight for you against your enemies to save you.*

Today I am in the fight of my life for the ministry. I am surrounded with offended people because I am working for a God of excellence. Therefore, I feel the burden that all that we do must be our best. Many do not do their best. They do just enough to get by.

Ask yourself today, "Am I a person who tries daily to do my best?" God expects us to be examples of his excellence. The world will see this in you, and it will set you apart. Be prepared though, for the attack when people you depend on do not live in excellence. The enemy will have you misinterpreted and mocked, but God will save you!

Dear God, please forgive me first. Then Lord, please let others see you in me as I take my life in ministry a direct representation of you. Lord, please fight my enemies because I can't. I love you. Amen.

Deuteronomy 23:14

*For the Lord your God walks in the midst of your camp to deliver you and to give up your enemies before you.*

God literally walks in your life. He knows exactly where you are. Again, the enemy loves to lie to us frequently in times of despair telling us that God is no where to be found. The enemy tells us that God does not even know who we are. He tells us that if God were around, then why are we in this mess.

Today, speak this verse over repeatedly. God will deliver you. Then, He will bring your enemies to you. WHOA! We will have God not only defend and deliver us, but He gives your enemies before you.

Dear God, forgive me that I give up on you so easily. Forgive me for falling into the enemy's trap of thinking you are no where. Lord, let me feel your presence as you deliver me and defend me today. I love you. Amen.

<u>Deuteronomy 30:7</u>
*And the Lord your God will put all these curses upon your enemies and on those who hate you, who persecute you.*

I know it is not nice for me to relish in this scripture but sometimes the pain of my broken hearts are too much to bear. Then I reflect on this scripture, and my heart lightens. My hope is lifted just knowing that my pain does not go unnoticed with God. That the people who hurt me, lie about me, and criticize me will one day answer for this.

First though, I have to make sure that I am in alignment with God and that their words have no truth. Then I ask God to forgive me and then forgive my enemies. I can rest in the nugget of truth that He knows it all and He will be a God of justice in the end.

Dear God, forgive me. Lord, forgive my enemies. Help me today as I search for you that I feel your presence in the knowledge that you will handle my enemies and you will defend me. I love you. Amen.

Joshua 21:44
*The Lord gave them rest round about, just as He had sworn to their fathers. Not one of all their enemies withstood them; the Lord delivered all their enemies into their hands.*

I think this is what most of us miss most, is rest and sleep. I once had someone very spiritual ask me, "How well are you sleeping?" I soon found out that we as children of God should be able to leave it all with God, our burdens, worries, and anxiety at his feet and find rest and sleep.

My question to you is this today, "How well are you sleeping or how rested do you really feel?" Ask God to help you learn to lay your cares at his feet as often in a day as you need so that you can find rest in the Lord.

Dear God, I am so tired. I am not sleeping well, and my mind races all day everyday. Lord, let me feel your presence today as I learn to lay it all down one by one my worries of this day. Lord, I release these to you so that I may rest in you. I love you.

<u>2 Samuel 7:1</u>
*When King David dwelt in his house and*
*the Lord had given him rest from all his*
*surrounding enemies,*

I am learning to ask God for my rest. With
the fast paced world and all of the deadlines
and work loads, we really need some rest.
I ask God what I need to let go of in my
schedule. Is there anything that is taking
time from my day that is not necessary?

Today, breathe in and breathe out slowly.
Feel the movement of air that releases. Do
this with God and your petitions in prayer
for rest and release. Ask him to show you
what it is that you could let go in your
schedule to free you up just a little more.

Dear God, I ask you to help me release to
you my cares. Lord, I breathe in and out and
ask you to show up and help me find peace
in you. Lord, reveal to me anything that
could be removed from my schedule so that
I may have more time to find rest in you. I
love you. Amen.

<u>2 Samuel 22:4</u>
*I call on the Lord, Who is worthy to be praised, and I am saved from my enemies.*

Don't ever hesitate to call upon the Lord in times of need. He is there. You don't have to hide from him when you are sitting in your own mess. He already knows what you have done. There is nothing we can hide from God.

Call upon God whenever you need him. He will be there in so many ways. He will save you from despair. He will heal your broken heart. He will give you hope by showing you the light at the end of the tunnel. Praise and thank him today for always rescuing us from our enemies even if we provoked it ourselves.

Dear God, I call upon you today to help me. I need your grace and mercy and love in the only way you can give. Lord, I want to feel your presence as I see you remove the enemy from my life. I love you. Amen.

<u>2 Kings 17:39</u>
*But the Lord your God you shall*
*[reverently] fear; then He will deliver you*
*out of the hands of all your enemies.*

We are to deeply, respectfully fear God.
No, God is not a God of fears, but He
is worthy to be feared. He is the God of
Justice. He is the God of all creation. We
must all reverently fear him before we can
know him.

Don't let the enemy deceive you into
thinking that this is incongruent to what
God stands for. That is a lie. Before you
can know God intimately, you must first
recognize who He is and fear that He is the
all in all.

Dear God, I recognize you today as the
creator of the entire universe. Lord, I stand
in awe of your creation. Lord, forgive me
in not addressing the power and might you
are. Lord, let me feel your presence today
as I reverently and respectfully bow to you.
I love you. Amen.

*Day 342*

<u>Psalm 18:3</u>
*I will call upon the Lord, Who is to be praised; so shall I be saved from my enemies.*

I think what amazes me today in our scripture is how many times God says this repeatedly. God says, I will save you, rescue, you, deliver you, and hear you. Why don't we get that? Why don't we internalize this to our core that God is there just for us!

The enemy plays these things in our minds. You did this yourself. God can't help you. You are a sinner. You messed this up, and God can't hear you. These are all lies from the enemy. God already knows what we have done, and He knows we will never be perfect. Today, make God the first person you call upon and then praise him for being there.

Dear God, help me to bind the enemy. Help me through the blood of Christ break free from shame. Lord let me feel your presence today as I call upon you and thank you for always being there for me. I love you. Amen.

<u>Psalm 54:5</u>
*He will pay back evil to my enemies; in Your faithfulness [Lord] put an end to them.*

As I have said earlier, sometimes in this life we will never see our enemies sweat or pay a price. But we must know, as the scripture states, that God is faithful, and He will repay our enemies for us.

God will put an end to the fight we are fighting. God will pay back the evil to your enemies. Just remember it may not be in this lifetime. God is a God of justice, and He will make all of those who do evil pay for it.

Dear God, please forgive me. Lord, forgive my enemies for they really don't even know who I am. Forgive those that break my heart. Lord, let me feel you today as I release those who have hurt me to you so that you can repay them one day for the wounds they caused. I love you. Amen.

Psalm 54:7

*For He has delivered me out of every trouble, and my eye has looked [in triumph] on my enemies.*

I love this because it says, has delivered me out of every trouble. It didn't say some troubles. It says He delivered him out of every trouble. David is my favorite person in the Bible. He gives me such hope that God is every-thing we read in scriptures.

David committed adultery, committed murder, and he was always getting himself into trouble. He also had a lot of enemies. BUT God, He looks at our hearts not what we do in sin. God saw David as a man after God's own heart. As I write this today, tears flow down my cheeks, because I have failed God in many ways, but I love him so much. He knows that.

Dear God, forgive me a sinner. Lord, I know I mess things up all the time. Lord, let me feel you today as you console me and comfort me as I cry tears of love for you. Draw close to me today, I love you. Amen.

Psalm 59:10
*My God in His mercy and steadfast*
*love will meet me; God will let me look*
*[triumphantly] on my enemies (those who*
*lie in wait for me).*

You can count on God for, if you truly are
in alignment with God, He will never let you
look like a fool! God will not be mocked.
Our lives are a direct reflection of who God
is. Our lives represent God here on earth.
God will never let his children look like
fools and defeated to our enemies.

God has proven this to me so many times.
Even though the enemy tries to get me to
fold and surrender to those that make fun of
me, I stand firm knowing God will help me
come out triumphantly. Those who plan for
my demise and failure will not ever get the
chance to defeat me!

Dear God, thank you that your mercy and
steadfast love cover me from my enemies.
Lord, thank you for your presence today
as I leave this time with you knowing I am
triumphant in Christ. I love you. Amen.

Psalm 78:53
*And He led them on safely and in confident trust, so that they feared not; but the sea overwhelmed their enemies.*

Some times, we are not quite sure how God will handle our enemies. He may wait until the judgment day or He may choose to make them pay on earth. Sometimes we will see our enemies suffer for the wrong or offense that they have caused.

Don't get discouraged today though if you don't see the way God deals with your enemies. I have found out most evil that people do in the end they know what they have caused. It goes back to the mirror theory I have, "What does the mirror tell you who you are, good or bad, drawing closer or farther from God, a server of man or God?" Then ask God to not let the mirror lie to you.

Dear God, I stand before you in the mirror. Lord, show your presence today as you reveal to me the things that are not of you. Help me to be a pure image for you. I love you. Amen.

<u>Psalm 138:7</u>
*Though I walk in the midst of trouble, You will revive me; You will stretch forth Your hand against the wrath of my enemies, and Your right hand will save me.*

Specifically today, I need revived. The enemy is really working overtime on one of my teenagers. I pray, I cover with the blood, I confess, and I bring him to the altar before God, but the enemy is relentless.

Lord, please renew and activate my faith in you. I am weary from the fighting. I am weary from the injustice. Lord, I know you are in control, but this is so painful. I am left with nothing. All I can do is watch my child stumble and suffer the consequences. Please Lord, stretch out your hand and save me and my son.

Dear God, I am in the midst of trouble, and I have no where else to go but you. Lord, please stretch forth your hand over the enemy and save my son and me. I love you. Amen.

<u>Proverbs 16:7</u>
*When a man's ways please the Lord, He makes even his enemies to be at peace with him.*

Lord, I pray today that my enemies have peace with me. Lord, I know that they can be relentless to try and cause me to stumble. Lord, I hope my ways are pleasing to you. I hope that I am in right standing through the blood of Christ.

Lord, show me if I need to realign anything for you. Lord, help me to see what my enemies are doing. Thank you that you even cause my enemies to quit fighting with me because you have made peace between them and me.

Dear God, I need you to help me stay pleasing in your sight. Lord, show your presence to me today as I search my heart for anything that might cause me to stumble in your sight. Lord, thank you for making my enemies have peace with me. I love you. Amen.

Isaiah 30:25
*And upon every high mountain and upon
every high hill there will be brooks and
streams of water in the day of the great
slaughter [the day of the Lord], when
the towers fall [and all His enemies are
destroyed]*

This just shows us again that there is an
end to this world. There will be a day that
will be the last on earth. God says here that
the highest mountains will have brooks and
streams of water to wash away the blood of
the slaughtered evil doers.

Ask yourself if you are ready for the end
day. Are you prepared for today to be your
last? If not, go to God today and tell him
you need him. Confess your sins, and make
him the Lord of your heart.

Dear God, please don't let me die. Don't
allow me to lie to myself any longer. Show
your presence to me, Lord, as I make
adjustments in my life to make you my
Lord and Savior. I love you. Amen.

<u>Nahum 1:2</u>
*The Lord is a jealous God and avenging;*
*the Lord avenges and He is full of*
*wrath. The Lord takes vengeance on His*
*adversaries and reserves wrath for His*
*enemies.*

This reminds me of my teenage love affairs
when thought jealousy was a way to show
our love for one another. God is a jealous
lover. God does not want anything to come
first in our lives BUT him.

We need to make sure God sees in our
hearts that He is our first love. Look and see
if you are doing all you can to make God
first in your life. The best way to insure that
your day is the way God designed is to give
God your first minutes of the day. Find time
to be still and read God's word, so He will
need not be jealous.

Dear God, please forgive me for not making
you first everyday. Please help me to make
you my first love of every day. Lord, let
me feel your presence today as a lover who
wants no other but you. I love you. Amen.

<u>Zechariah 9:15</u>
*The Lord of hosts shall defend and protect them; and they shall devour and they shall tread on [their fallen enemies] as on slingstones [that have missed their aim], and they shall drink [of victory] and be noisy and turbulent as from wine and become full like bowls [used to catch the sacrificial blood], like the corners of the [sacrificial] altar.*

The Lord again shows He will defend us. He will protect us from the enemy. God will allow us to tread on our enemies; he will not let the enemy win.

The Lord will celebrate with us on the judgment day. I like to compare it to a birthday party for a loved one. That is how the last day will be for God's children, a celebration of eternal life in heaven.

Dear God, thank you for being my defender. Lord, help me to see my enemies one day get your justice. Lord, forgive me and let me feel you as the comfort of knowing you are my protection fills my heart.

Mark 12:36
*David himself, [inspired] in the Holy
Spirit, declared, The Lord said to my Lord,
Sit at My right hand until I make Your
enemies [a footstool] under Your feet.*

Just imagine all the people who have hurt
you. Think of all the ways the enemy has
tried to take your life off of God's course.
Then envision yourself sitting in a big,
comfortable chair when God places a
footstool at your feet. Wait. The footstool is
your enemies at your feet.

God is so fair. He knows what the enemy
has thrown at you. He knows the cunning
ways he seduces us to sin. But God always
delivers us. So, next time you are offended
or wounded just remember that one day
they will be a footstool under your feet.

Dear God, thank you for the last Day of
Judgment. Thank you that you know the
enemies ploys to entertain us to sin. Lord,
help me feel you to day as I relish in the
day that my enemies will be a footstool
under my feet. I love you. Amen.

<u>Genesis 15:1</u>
*After these things, the word of the Lord came to Abram in a vision, saying, Fear not, Abram, I am your Shield, your abundant compensation, and your reward shall be exceedingly great.*

I love God's economy. The world's economy has nothing to do with God's economy. What God rewards us with has far greater value than money. God's compensation and rewards are always exceedingly great.

When our own children are doing what is right and good, we love to give gifts that are great. God is the same way. He loves to give to his children eternal gifts.

Dear God, thank you that you are my shield. You are a God that rewards those who do well. Lord, as I come to you as a child and you as my Father, I ask to feel your presence as child that waits on a huge gift with hope and anticipation. I love you. Amen.

## 2 Samuel 22:36
*You have also given me the shield of Your salvation; and Your condescension and gentleness have made me great.*

I don't know about you, but I had to look up the meaning of condescension in the dictionary. It means voluntary assumption of equality with a person regarded as inferior. In other words, God tries to be at our side even though we are far more inferior to him.

God truly is so gentle. The enemy tries to make us feel that God sits up on a throne waiting to punish us. Just the opposite is true. God yearns to touch us, bless us, favor us, and deliver us. Will you allow him to walk alongside of you?

Dear God, help me to clean my life up and to surrender to you today. Lord, I long to be right with you all the time. Lord, let me feel you as we spend more time together and allow my heart to feel your gentle touch. I love you. Amen.

<u>Psalm 3:3</u>
*But You, O Lord, are a shield for me, my glory, and the lifter of my head.*

Have you ever been so low that you didn't want to lift your head? I have been so down that I literally did not want to lift my head up to get out of bed. The good news is that God is there to lift us up when we can't on our own.

Go to God today and allow him to spiritually lift you. Ask him to give you a new sense of hope and encouragement so that your head will be easy to keep lifted. Ask the Lord to lessen your load so that you will not have to bear so many burdens alone.

Dear God, please help me to lift my spirits. Lord, the world can be so depressing. Lord, help me to feel you lift me up so I have a new spring in my step. I love you. Amen.

<u>Psalm 7:10</u>
*My defense and shield depend on God,*
*Who saves the upright in heart.*

My defense solely relies on God. I am naked without him. He is my defender and the only one who is always healing my heart. I am sure that my dependence on him is much better than any other dependence down here on earth.

Who do you depend on in times of trouble? Who do you feel is your defender? God has taught me through many heartaches that He is the one and only one I can truly depend on. Have you made this assessment for your own life? If not, claim God as your total defender and shield and the only one to be trusted.

Dear God, today I feel your presence as I stand here knowing there is none like you. You are my sole defender. You are the only one I can depend on all the time everyday. Thank you Lord, for being my shield, defender, and the only one that I know will be there. I love you. Amen.

Psalm 119:114
*You are my hiding place and my shield; I hope in Your word.*

In times of tears, I go to God and tell him that He is your hiding place. Many times God is the only place I know to run. He is the only one with ears that are listening. He is the only one that really cares at all. So, I go to him and hide. I tell him all of my secrets and my disappointments.

Have you ever called God your hiding place? If not, today go and get still and just ask God to show up and listen. Tell him all that you are felling, and He will be there in your time of need.

Dear God, you are my hiding place. You are the only one who really listens and cares. Lord, I know you have plans for me, and I come to you in silence and hide within your walls. Let me feel your presence as I tell you all my needs, disappointments, and fears. I love you. Amen.

<u>Psalm 121:5</u>
*The Lord is your keeper; the Lord is your shade on your right hand [the side not carrying a shield].*

This just proves to me even when we can't defend ourselves or don't know how to defend ourselves, God is ready and willing to defend our weakness. Here we see that God is covering the part where there is no covering.

Many of us need this affirmation. God is there defending us when we don't even know how to defend ourselves or when we are too weak to do it. God is our defender at all times. He truly is watching us all the time and calls himself our keeper.

Dear God, thank you for defending me even when I don't know how to defend myself or when I am too weak to try. Lord, I feel your presences as I know deep within my heart you not only are my defender but the keeper of my life. I love you. Amen.

<u>Proverbs 2:7</u>
*He hides away sound and godly Wisdom
and stores it for the righteous (those who
are upright and in right standing with
Him); He is a shield to those who walk
uprightly and in integrity,*

It is amazing how God literally pours
out his wisdom to those who are in right
standing with him. In this world today, we
all need his Godly wisdom and revelations
to survive the chaos and confusion.

Integrity is a characteristic that has been
lost since the beginning of time. Integrity
is something even secular minded people
notice. The definition is adherence to moral
and ethical principles; soundness of moral
character; honesty. Could you be described
as any of these terms?

Dear God, I need your Godly wisdom and
sound mind. Please let me feel you today
as I find a new sense of ideas and thoughts.
Lord, help me be a person of integrity and in
right standing with you. I love you. Amen.

Exodus 31:3
*And I have filled him with the Spirit of God,
in wisdom and ability, in understanding
and intelligence, and in knowledge, and in
all kinds of craftsmanship,*

When God comes into your life,
transformation is seen from the inside out.
You have a keen sense of wisdom. You
better understand motivations and thought
processes of man. You just are more
enlightened to the meaning of life, but you
also become better at your gifting.

Today, if you are a teacher, God can
make you a better one. If you are a nurse,
God can make you more caring. If you
are a cabinet maker, you can become
the best cabinet maker. Once God enters
your life, all things become enlightened,
strengthened, and improved.

Dear God, thank you for the gift of your
Spirit which dwells within us. Thank you
that you make us so much wiser, insightful,
and better at our jobs. I love you. Amen.

2 Chronicles 1:12
*Wisdom and knowledge are granted you.*
*And I will give you riches, possessions,*
*honor, and glory, such as none of the kings*
*had before you, and none after you shall*
*have their equal.*

God just waits to grant us our desires.
Then on top of that, He longs to shower us
with gifts. We don't hear enough of this in
our churches. We don't see this side of God
often enough. He waits to give us finer
gifts than Kings receive.

God acts just like our parents when we
accomplish goals, like graduating from
High School; a treasured and special gift
is usually given. God is the same way. He
longs to reward us and grant us knowledge
and wisdom. What more could we want
from God?

Dear God, I am so glad in this revelation
today. I feel your presence with a new
sense of hope that you really enjoy giving
us not only what we need, but elaborate
gifts. I love you. Amen.

Job 12:13
*But [only] with [God] are [perfect]*
*wisdom and might; He [alone] has [true]*
*counsel and understanding.*

God alone is perfect in wisdom,
knowledge, and understanding. There
is no other substitute for him. We must
discipline our minds and hearts to go to
God for counsel. We all are so quick to run
to a friend, a mate, or family member in
times of need, but we must learn to go to
God first.

Today, when an appropriate time appears,
don't turn to a friend. Go straight to God.
Make a commitment to yourself to just
go to God first for all of your decisions
and solutions. You will be amazed at how
quickly God answers and gives great
counsel and comfort.

Dear God, you are perfect. Thank you that
you do want to help me and counsel me.
Lord, let me feel your presence today as I
turn to you for solutions and ideas. I love
you. Amen.

<u>Job 28:23</u>
*God understands the way [to Wisdom] and He knows the place of it [Wisdom is with God alone].*

The good word today is that there are answers for all of us and all of our needs. There is a place that we can go in order to find wisdom and answers. God creates a place just for us to come, seek, and find wisdom.

God will show this to us if we allow him to. He will make a way for us to find what we need if we seek him. There is a place to find all of our answers. Is right there in front of us, God.

Dear God, I do have so many needs that must get answered. My children, ministry, and family members need my solutions and counsel. Lord, I seek your way to wisdom. Lord, I long to feel your presence to day as solutions and comfort are revealed to me through you. I love you. Amen.

<u>Proverbs 1:7</u>
*The reverent and worshipful fear of the Lord is the beginning and the principal and choice part of knowledge [its starting point and its essence]; but fools despise skillful and godly Wisdom, instruction, and discipline.*

The best place to start your EVERY day is to worship with reverent fear of the Lord. This sounds impossible, but it is so simple. When your eyes open in the first second of the day, before your feet hit the floor, say, "Lord, you are the beginning and the end. You are in control of every area of my life."

Forgive me Lord, today of any failures and forgive others that hurt me. Lord, you obviously have a purpose for me today. Otherwise, I would be in a casket. Reveal to me what you need me to do or say that will help the Kingdom today. Lord, make me an example to all showing who you are. I give you all the glory for what you are and do for me today! I love you. Amen.

<u>Proverbs 1:23</u>
*If you will turn (repent) and give heed to my reproof, behold, I [Wisdom] will pour out my spirit upon you, I will make my words known to you.*

I had to face this scripture today in a way that I did not want. God has been working on one area of my life that borders on disobedience. I realized that I had continued a destructive behavior that was not very Christ-like, and I had been justifying my actions.

Literally today, as I was finishing this book, God asked me in our quiet time to lay down something in my life. God showed me that I must repent of a particular weakness. I thought I had already done so, but I had not really.

God revealed to me that to repent means to turn away from and not do anymore. So, I had to confess to God today and tell him from this point forward I would turn away from this behavior.

*Day 365*

What do you need to repent from today? Allow God to help you so you can have his spirit poured all over you.

Dear God, I repent today to never go back and to really change my actions. Help me today as I find strength to be obedient so more of you can be seen in me. I love you. Amen.

**Laine Lawson Craft** is a gifted and insightful speaker who communicates a contagious hope. Her "God can move your mountain" testimony inspires listeners to conquer their difficult circumstances by surrendering to God, trusting that God can do the impossible, and to build a deeper intimacy with God. Broken hearts are healed, faith is activated, hope is found again, and a new sense of belonging to a community of believers is developed.

Laine has been hand picked by God, and she walks out the steps of obeying God by sharing all over the world what God has done in her life. Laine has been in full-time ministry since 2007 which has led her to develop a number of opportunities that allow her to share her journey with Christ.

She began as a public speaker and founder of WHOA Ministries, Women Who Hear, Obey and Act on the Word of God. Through that ministry, she founded the Brown Bag Bible Buddies, has become the Publisher of WHOA Women Magazine, Host of the WHOA Talk Show that airs on WAPT - the ABC affiliate for the Mid-Mississippi market, and President of WHOA Publishing.

Laine has been married for more than 23 years and has three beautiful children, Steven, 19, Lawson, 16, and Kaylee, 15. Laine loves her family deeply and enjoys being a Mom. She loves to share her testimony in word and fun.

Laine can be seen on the WHOA Show television broadcasts on Sunday at 10:30 a.m. on WAPT or online at: www.whoaministries.com.

She can be heard personally at one of the three satellites of Brown Bag Bible Buddies which meets on the third Thursday of every month in the Jackson Mississippi Metro Area. Through these and other venues, Laine shares how God has used the many trials in her life to begin the process of conforming her to His image. And her life is truly an example of how God does do the impossible today and how the underdog can win with God. She firmly believes there is no condemnation for those who love the Lord, and that no sin, no shame, NOTHING can separate us from the love of Christ. God is always there and waiting on us. He is God who never gives up on us!

For more information on Laine Lawson Craft, please visit: whoaministries.com, lainelawsoncraft.com, or email her at: lainecraft@lainecraft.net